Green Cuisine

The Organic Vegetable Cookbook

Anna Ross

©1999 Green Peppercorn

Illustrations by Howard Vause

Printed by APB Colour Print Ltd, Bristol

ISBN 0 9536446 0 X

Published by Green Peppercorn
20 Wellington Hill, Bristol, BS7 8SR
Telephone: 0117 952 3055
email: green.peppercorn@iname.com

Order your copy by credit card on 0117 952 3055 or
Send us a cheque made payable to A Ross
for £9.99 (includes £2 postage and packing).

Contents

Author's Note

I have been researching and writing this book for the past two years and have been encouraged and influenced by friends who are committed to buying organic products. Thank you. This is reflected not only in the simplicity and range of recipes but also the inclusion of many dinner party dishes. It has also kept the focus on using the staple vegetables available and the more unusual. Here are some ideas for what you do with that strange knobbly thing.

For Janet, Fred, Clare and Anne.

Introduction

Why buy this book?

Why do you need an organic vegetable cookbook? How does this book differ from Delia *et al.*, the TV Ready Steady Cookbooks and the current trend for food in a flash?

This book is full of recipes that are tailored specifically to the organic vegetable market. These recipes cover the 32 most readily available organic vegetables, from the shops or homegrown, and recognise that a weekly purchase or box delivery will always include carrots, potatoes and greens. We need both traditional and new ways of eating our greens (and aubergines, avocados, beetroots and so on). Especially as they taste so much better than their non-organic alternatives.

Carrots, onions and potatoes are the organic staples - and the cheapest. Traditional vegetables like turnips, parsnips and beetroots are readily available. You will discover new ways of cooking all of these vegetables.

Knobbly Roots

Although the variety of organic vegetables available is a bit more restricted than the full range of non-organic vegetables we also see the appearance of new, strange looking, knobbly roots - celeriac, Jerusalem artichokes - and the smooth, white kohlrabi. This book will give you more ideas of how to cook the unusual organic vegetables.

Here is an easy reference to reach for when you wonder what to do with the umpteenth cabbage, carrot and courgette or you are not sure of your celeriac, or you've run out of ideas for fennel. This book contains over 130 recipe ideas for everyday cooking using widely available organic ingredients. There is not much call for cranberries, miso, tahini, tamari or saffron here. But delicious, nutritious and interesting meal ideas.

Organic For All

I recognise the need for quick meals and the health benefits of eating less fat and more fibre. Less cooking retains more nutrients and highlights the need for recipes that include as many raw or quick-cooked vegetables as possible - yes you can grate a new, baby turnip for a salad.

This book is not only for vegetarians. These recipes can be served to accompany meat or fish dishes as well as vegetarian main courses.

As someone who has eaten organic food for a long time I am delighted that the range of food is expanding so rapidly to include not only the basic ingredients of milk, yoghurt, flour, pasta, rice but also organic Parmesan, noodles, olive oil, herbs, nuts and tinned and frozen vegetables. The overwhelming majority of the ingredients that I use here can be bought in their fresh, organic form so that these recipes are 100% organic. If you grow your own then so much the better, you can pick and eat within hours.

A note for parents wanting to produce organically reared children: Alice (7 months) will eat most things puréed and Freddie (2 years) will even eat beetroot soup.

Scary Food

In the wake of BSE, e-coli and GM food scares the market for organic food continues to grow rapidly. The UK organic food market is now worth about £350 million, more than three times what it was worth in 1993. The Soil Association is the charity which promotes organic food and farming, and enforces organic food standards. They suggest consumers believe that organic food is the only food they can trust. Organic food contains no pesticides, no 'nasties', no toxins and is GM-free. It also tastes better, is fresher, has more flavour and more texture than its chemically grown neighbour. According to Lynda Brown, author of "The Shopper's Guide To Organic Food" (Fourth Estate, £7.99), an organic carrot has spent an extra three weeks in the ground, taken up water more slowly and developed a higher fibre content. That is why, compared to its watery, chemical counterpart, an organic carrot tastes sweeter.

Why Eat Organic?

The Soil Association booklet "Where to Buy Organic Food" (Soil Association, £4.50), stresses the many important beneficial effects of organic food and farming. Strict animal welfare rules apply to livestock production; food will not have been treated with noxious chemicals; organic farming is better for the environment; and the routine use of antibiotics is not permitted. Human health benefits too, as organic food has been shown to have more vitamins and trace elements than conventionally grown food.

The Soil Association is working with farmers to convert to organic methods and receives thousands of calls a year from those enquiring how to convert. Farmers have been persuaded by continual food scares that consumer demand for organic food will continue to grow. And the figures support this with Soil Association estimates of an annual market growth of 40%. By 2002 organic food will account for around 8% of the total food market and be worth more than £1 billion.

Who eats organic?

The stereotype of an organic vegetable buyer as a health freak hippie no longer applies. A huge range of people now buy organic food and even those who don't buy it for themselves are buying it for their children - one in four children eat organic products regularly. Organic supermarkets are opening and traditional supermarkets are continually increasing their organic ranges to catch a fast moving bandwagon.

It is now possible to eat almost 100% organic food. Prices which were once double that of non-organic food are falling fast as the market becomes increasingly competitive. At Waitrose, recently voted the Organic Supermarket of the Year, the premium is on average seven per cent (at Asda and Safeway it's twenty per cent). The cheapest option is often an organic box scheme and it's delivered to your door. 50,000 families and 30 per cent of organic growers in the UK are now involved in these box schemes. They are generally more committed to using UK suppliers. A recent development in organic selling is the local farmers' market set up with the support of local councils. These too, tend to be cheaper than supermarkets and only sell food that is grown locally.

Local health food shops stock a wide range of organic food and often a good variety of organic vegetables. It is even possible to order organic food via the internet. So, however you shop, you can buy the organic ingredients in these recipes.

Aubergine

Once regarded as a rather exotic vegetable, aubergines are now readily available. If you grow your own, this plant does need pampering and will generally fail unless in a greenhouse.

Salting used to be recommended to reduce bitterness but today's varieties are rarely bitter. However, salting does draw out moisture and reduce the amount of oil soaked up during cooking. To salt, place the slices into a colander, sprinkle with salt and leave to drain for one hour. Rinse well and pat dry.

Aubergine Soufflé

Serves 4   Preparation 35 minutes   Cooking time 50 minutes

2 large aubergines

1 garlic clove

2 tsp fresh thyme

2 tbsp yoghurt

50g (2oz) Parmesan cheese

4 large eggs

For the white sauce:

15g (½oz) margarine

1 tbsp flour

150ml (5fl oz) milk

Salt and pepper

1. Place the aubergines on a baking tray and bake whole at 180ºC (350ºF) Mark 4 for 35 minutes until soft. Leave to cool.

2. Melt the margarine, add the flour and cook, stirring for 1 minute. Slowly add the milk and continue stirring until the sauce thickens. Season with salt and pepper and simmer gently for 5 minutes.

3. Scoop out the aubergine flesh and mix with the crushed garlic, chopped thyme leaves, yoghurt and half of the grated Parmesan. Mix into the white sauce.

4. Separate the eggs and stir the yolks into the aubergine mixture. Beat the egg whites until stiff and fold into the aubergine mixture.

5. Grease a large soufflé dish and pour in the soufflé mixture. Sprinkle with the remaining Parmesan and bake at 220ºC (425ºF) Mark 7 for 15-20 minutes. Serve immediately.

1

Aubergine & Tomato Tart

Serves 6   Preparation 25 minutes   Cooking time 45 minutes

For the shortcrust pastry:

175g (6oz) plain flour

Pinch of salt

75g (3oz) margarine

2 tbsp cold water

For the filling:

350g (12oz) aubergines

2 garlic cloves

2 tbsp olive oil

3 medium tomatoes

2 tbsp fresh basil

3 eggs

150ml (5fl oz) milk

50g (2oz) cheddar cheese

Salt and pepper

1. Sift the flour and salt into a bowl. Cut the margarine into small pieces and rub into the flour until the mixture resembles fine breadcrumbs. Add 2 tablespoons of cold water to mix to a firm dough, then wrap in cling film and chill for 30 minutes.

2. Meanwhile to prepare the filling, chop the aubergines into 2cm (1 inch) chunks, mix with the crushed garlic, olive oil and season with salt and pepper. Bake at 200°C (400°F) Mark 6 for 15-20 minutes until tender.

3. Roll out the pastry on a lightly floured surface to line a 20cm (8 inch) flan dish. Prick entire surface with a fork and bake blind at 200°C (400°F) Mark 6 for 15 minutes until just firm to the touch.

4. Beat the eggs, milk and cheese together and season with salt and pepper. Chop the tomatoes into 1cm (½ inch) chunks and arrange in the pastry case with the aubergines. Sprinkle over the roughly chopped basil. Pour over the egg mixture and bake at 200°C (400°F) Mark 6 for 30 minutes until set.

Aubergine & Tomato Pasta Sauce

Serves 4   Preparation 15 minutes   Cooking time 30 minutes

2 medium aubergines

3 tbsp olive oil

4 tbsp red wine

1 medium onion

2 garlic cloves

2 x 400g (14oz) cans tomatoes

Salt and pepper

2 tbsp double cream

3 tbsp fresh marjoram

1. Cut the aubergine into 1cm (½ inch) cubes and sauté in hot oil for 5 minutes. Add the red wine and simmer for a further 15 minutes.

2. Meanwhile, chop the onion, crush the garlic and sauté until the onion is transparent. Add to the aubergine mixture along with the chopped tomatoes. Season with salt and pepper and simmer for 10 minutes.

3. Remove the pan from the heat and stir in the cream and chopped marjoram.

4. Serve with freshly cooked penne.

Avocado

An avocado is never ripe when you want it to be. The constant prodding they receive on a supermarket shelf, by shoppers looking for a perfect specimen, often leads to bruising. They are one of the few fruits that contain fat but they are also rich in vitamins C and E.

Avocado dip or Guacamole is a Mexican recipe made hot and spicy by adding chillies and usually served with tacos. To slice finely for a salad, halve the avocado, remove the stone and slice with the skin still on. Then remove the skin.

Avocado, Tomato & Feta Salad

Serves 4   Preparation 15 minutes

1 lettuce

2 large tomatoes

1 large avocado

200g (7oz) feta cheese

20 black olives

2 tbsp fresh thyme

For the dressing:

2 tbsp red wine vinegar

6 tbsp olive oil

Salt and pepper

1. Wash and finely chop the lettuce. Thinly slice the tomatoes. Chop and peel the avocado. Mix together in a large serving bowl.

2. Crumble the feta cheese and add to the salad along with the olives and chopped fresh thyme.

3. For the dressing, combine the vinegar and oil in a screw-topped jar, season with salt and pepper and shake vigorously. Pour over the salad.

Avocado Dip

Serves 6
Preparation 10 minutes

2 large avocados
1 dried red chilli
3 tbsp lemon juice
1 garlic clove
2 tbsp olive oil
3 tomatoes
Salt and pepper

1. Peel and roughly chop the avocados and place in a liquidiser. Add the finely chopped chilli, lemon juice, crushed garlic, and olive oil and blend until smooth.

2. Finely chop the tomatoes and add to the avocado mixture. Season with salt and pepper.

Chilled Avocado Soup

Serves 6   Preparation 10 minutes   Cooking time 20 minutes

1 onion
2 medium potatoes
2 tbsp oil
900ml (1½ pints) vegetable stock
2 large avocados
Juice of 1 lemon
2 tbsp fresh dill
Salt and pepper

1. Roughly chop the onion and potatoes and sauté in the hot oil until the onion is transparent.

2. Add the stock, bring to the boil, cover and simmer for 20 minutes until tender. Cool slightly and transfer to a liquidiser.

3. Peel and chop the avocados and add to the liquidiser with the lemon juice. Blend until smooth.

4. Season with salt and pepper and transfer to a bowl. Cover and chill for several hours.

5

Beetroot

Beetroots add a beautiful colour and flavour to salads and hot dishes. Bortsch, an Eastern European soup, is a glorious pink colour. Our illustration was painted with a beetroot.

Before cooking, wash beetroots in cold water with the leaf stalks and root intact. Don't remove the skin as bleeding results in a loss of colour and flavour. After boiling, you can rub the skin off.

Beetroot leaves are very nutritious (high in vitamins A and C) and you can cook them in the same way as spinach.

Beetroot & Onion Tart

Serves 6   Preparation 30 minutes   Cooking time 95 minutes

500g (1lb) beetroot

350g (12oz) small onions

2 tbsp oil

75g (3oz) caster sugar

250g (8oz) puff pastry

2 tbsp balsamic vinegar

Salt and pepper

1. Wash the beetroot. Place in a pan of salted water and bring to the boil. Cover and simmer for 45 minutes until tender. Drain and allow to cool slightly. Peel and chop into 2cm (1 inch) pieces.

2. Meanwhile, peel and chop the onions into quarters. Add to another pan of boiling water and simmer for 10 minutes. Drain.

3. Spread the oil over a non-stick ovenproof frying pan. Sprinkle in the caster sugar and arrange beetroot and onion pieces evenly over the base. Season with salt and pepper. Cook on the hob for 15-20 minutes until the sugar has caramelised.

4. Roll out the pastry on a floured surface into a circle 5cm (2 inches) larger than the edge of the pan. Add the balsamic vinegar to the beetroot mixture. Cover the mixture with the pastry pushing the edge down so that it will form the edge of the tart when turned over.

5. Prick the pastry and bake in a preheated oven at 220ºC (425ºF) Mark 7 for 35 minutes until brown. Cool for 5 minutes and turn over onto a serving plate.

Bortsch

Serves 6   Preparation 20 minutes   Cooking time 60 minutes

500g (1lb) beetroot

1 large onion

500g (1lb) potatoes

2 tbsp oil

2 garlic cloves

1.2 litres (2 pints) vegetable stock / beetroot cooking liquid

2 tbsp lemon juice

Salt and pepper

150ml (5fl oz) thick yoghurt

1. Wash the beetroot and place in a pan of salted water, bring to the boil and simmer for 45 minutes until tender. Allow to cool slightly, peel and chop. Reserve cooking liquid.

2. Wash and chop the potatoes and peel and chop the onion. Sauté in hot oil for 10 minutes. Add the crushed garlic and cook for a further 5 minutes. Add the stock/cooking liquid, cover and simmer for 15 minutes until tender.

3. Add the beetroot and lemon juice to the pan, season with salt and pepper and continue cooking for 5 minutes.

4. Cool slightly, transfer to a liquidiser and blend until smooth. Reheat before serving, adding a swirl of yoghurt to each bowl.

Beetroot Salad

Serves 4
Preparation 10 minutes
Cooking time 45 minutes

500g (1lb) beetroot

1 bunch spring onions

240ml (8fl oz) yoghurt

1 tbsp fresh mint

1 tbsp lemon juice

Salt and pepper

1. Wash the beetroot, place in a pan of salted water, bring to the boil and simmer for 45 minutes until tender. Cool slightly, peel and dice.

2. Trim and slice the spring onions and mix with the beetroot.

3. Mix the yoghurt, chopped mint and lemon juice. Season with salt and pepper. Pour over the beetroot. Chill well before serving.

Beetroot & Rocket Couscous

Serves 4   Preparation 20 minutes   Cooking time 45 minutes

500g (1lb) beetroot

280g (10oz) couscous

600ml (1 pint) vegetable stock

75g (3oz) pine nuts

Juice of 1 lemon

4 tbsp olive oil

6 spring onions

50g (2oz) rocket leaves

Salt and pepper

1. Wash the beetroot. Place in a pan of salted water, bring to the boil, cover and simmer for 45 minutes until tender. Cool slightly, peel and chop into 2cm (1 inch) pieces.

2. Place the couscous in a large bowl and pour on the stock. When all the stock is absorbed stir gently with a fork. Leave to cool.

3. Dry-fry the pine nuts until golden. Cool and add to the couscous.

4. Add the lemon juice to the couscous along with the olive oil. Mix in the chopped spring onions, chopped rocket and beetroot. Season with salt and pepper.

Broad Beans

The broad bean, one of the oldest vegetables, would have been cultivated and cooked by Stone Age woman.

They are delicious when very fresh and you should avoid any with black blotches on the skin. Young beans have tender pods and you can treat them like french beans; top and tail and slice diagonally. You should shell more mature pods.

Steaming beans will retain their flavour and texture. You can cook the upper leaves like spinach.

Broad Bean & Courgette Pasta Sauce

Serves 4   Preparation 15 minutes   Cooking time 25 minutes

250g (8oz) shelled broad beans

1 garlic clove

1 medium onion

3 tbsp olive oil

2 medium courgettes

300ml (½ pint) single cream

1 x 400g (14oz) can tomatoes

100g (4oz) mozzarella cheese

Salt and pepper

1. Steam the broad beans for 10 minutes until just tender.

2. Slice the onion and sauté with the crushed garlic until the onion is transparent.

3. Cut the courgettes into 1cm (½ inch) slices and add to the pan. Cook for a further 5 minutes. Stir in the cream and the broad beans.

4. Add the chopped tomatoes and sliced mozzarella and heat gently. Season with salt and pepper.

5. Serve with freshly cooked penne.

Broad Bean Salad

Serves 4   Preparation 15 minutes   Cooking time 10 minutes

250g (8oz) shelled broad beans

1 lettuce

1 bunch spring onions

2 tbsp fresh parsley

2 medium tomatoes

For the dressing:

2 tbsp red wine vinegar

6 tbsp olive oil

1 tsp mustard

Salt and pepper

1. Steam the broad beans for ten minutes until tender. Leave to cool.

2. Shred the lettuce and mix with the chopped spring onions and chopped parsley. Slice the tomatoes and add to the salad.

3. Combine the dressing ingredients in a screw-topped jar and shake vigorously to mix. Pour over the salad and mix in the broad beans.

Broad Bean Soup

Serves 6   Preparation 15 minutes   Cooking time 35 minutes

750g (1½lb) shelled broad beans

2 medium onions

2 medium carrots

2 tbsp oil

1.5 litres (2½ pints) vegetable stock

3 tbsp fresh mint

Salt and pepper

1. Peel and chop the onions and carrots and sauté in the hot oil for 10-15 minutes.

2. Stir in the broad beans and stock, cover and simmer for 20 minutes. Season with salt and pepper.

3. Stir in the chopped mint, transfer to a liquidiser and blend until smooth.

Broccoli

Although these recipes use green broccoli (calabrese), you can use the purple sprouting varieties. These are the most popular for growing at home.

When preparing broccoli don't be tempted to cut off lots of stalk, just trim the ends and remove discoloured leaves. Cut thick stems lengthways.

This is another vegetable that you should steam to retain flavour and texture. You can serve it as a side dish with a knob of butter and a splash of lemon juice.

Stir-Fried Broccoli & Mushrooms

Serves 4   Preparation 15 minutes   Cooking time 8 minutes

500g (1lb) broccoli

500g (1lb) mushrooms

250g (8oz) carrots

1 bunch spring onions

1 garlic clove

4 tbsp oil

2 tbsp soy sauce

1 tbsp sesame oil

1. Cut the broccoli into small florets and slice the stems. Finely slice the mushrooms and cut the carrots into matchsticks.

2. Chop the spring onions, crush the garlic and stir-fry in hot oil for 2 minutes. Add the broccoli and carrots and stir-fry for a further 2 minutes.

3. Stir in the mushrooms (add extra oil if necessary) and fry for 2 minutes more.

4. Add the soy sauce and sherry and cook for 2 minutes. Stir in the sesame oil, season with pepper and remove from heat.

5. Serve with rice or noodles.

Braised Broccoli with Olives

Serves 4
Preparation 10 minutes
Cooking time 40 minutes

750g (1½lb) broccoli

2 garlic cloves

Juice of ½ a lemon

1 dried red chilli

3 tbsp olive oil

15 black olives

1. Cut the broccoli into large florets and place in a large, shallow frying pan. Crush the garlic and add to the pan along with the lemon juice and finely chopped chilli.

2. Stir in the olive oil and 150ml (5fl oz) of water. Cover and cook on a low heat for 40 minutes. Add the olives 5 minutes before the end.

Broccoli & Blue Cheese Quiche

Serves 6   Preparation 30 minutes   Cooking time 45 minutes

For the shortcrust pastry:

175g (6oz) plain flour

Pinch of salt

75g (3oz) margarine

2 tbsp cold water

For the filling:

500g (1lb) broccoli

125g (5oz) blue cheese

150ml (5fl oz) milk

3 eggs

1. Sift the flour and salt into a bowl. Cut the margarine into small pieces and rub into the flour until the mixture resembles fine breadcrumbs. Add 2 tablespoons

of cold water to mix to a firm dough, then wrap in cling film and chill for 30 minutes.

2. Meanwhile to prepare the filling, cut the broccoli into florets and steam for 10 minutes until just tender.

3. Roll out the pastry on a lightly floured surface to line a 20cm (8 inch) flan dish. Prick entire surface with a fork and bake blind at 200ºC (400ºF) Mark 6 for 15 minutes until just firm to the touch.

4. Arrange the broccoli in the pastry case and crumble the blue cheese on top. Beat the eggs with the milk and pour over the broccoli.

5. Bake at 200ºC (400ºF) Mark 6 for 35 minutes until set and browned.

Broccoli Pasta Sauce

Serves 4   Preparation 10 minutes   Cooking time 15 minutes

280g (10oz) broccoli

2cm (1 inch) piece root ginger

3 tbsp olive oil

175g (6oz) shelled peas

150ml (5fl oz) single cream

100g (4oz) ricotta cheese

Salt and pepper

1. Break the broccoli into small florets and finely slice the stems.

2. Grate the root ginger and fry with the broccoli for 5 minutes, stirring frequently.

3. Add the peas and continue to cook for 5 minutes.

4. Stir in the cream and cook gently for a further 5 minutes.

5. Add the ricotta cheese and season with salt and pepper. Serve with freshly cooked farfalle.

Broccoli & Cheese Soup

Serves 6   Preparation 15 minutes   Cooking time 30 minutes

2 medium potatoes

2 medium onions

2 tbsp oil

500g (1lb) broccoli

900 ml (1½ pints) vegetable stock

100g (4oz) cheddar cheese

150ml (5fl oz) milk or cream

Salt and pepper

1. Wash and chop the potatoes. Chop the onions and sauté with the potatoes in hot oil for 10 minutes.

2. Cut the broccoli into chunks (including stalks) and add to the pan with the vegetable stock. Bring to the boil, cover and simmer gently for 20 minutes.

3. Transfer to a liquidiser and blend until smooth. Add the grated cheese, salt and pepper and the milk. Reheat gently before serving.

Brussels Sprouts

Brussels sprouts were first grown in Belgium in the Middle Ages and have probably been disliked by many people ever since.

But, they do taste good in a stir-fry (being basically a baby cabbage) and, more traditionally, when served with sweet nuts such as almonds or chestnuts.

Small fresh sprouts can be shredded and served as part of a winter salad.

Stir-Fried Brussels with Ginger

Serves 4   Preparation 15 minutes   Cooking time 10 minutes

500g (1lb) Brussels sprouts

1 medium onion

2cm (1 inch) piece root ginger

2 garlic cloves

2 tbsp oil

1 medium orange

Salt and pepper

1. Wash, trim and shred the sprouts. Thinly slice the onion, finely chop the root ginger and the garlic.

2. Stir-fry the onion, garlic and ginger in hot oil for 3 minutes. Add the sprouts and continue to cook for a further 5 minutes.

3. Add the juice from the orange, cover and cook for 2 minutes until the vegetables are tender. Season with salt and pepper.

Brussels Sprouts with Parmesan

Serves 4
Preparation 10 minutes
Cooking time 10 minutes

500g (1lb) Brussels sprouts

50g (2oz) butter

2 garlic cloves

50g (2oz) Parmesan cheese

Salt and pepper

1. Wash and trim the sprouts, place in a pan of boiling water and cook for 5 minutes. Drain.

2. Melt the butter in a pan, add the crushed garlic and the sprouts. Season with salt and pepper and cook for a further 5 minutes.

3. Stir in the grated Parmesan just before serving.

Brussels Sprouts with Almonds

Serves 4   Preparation 10 minutes   Cooking time 10 minutes

500g (1lb) Brussels sprouts

25g (1oz) butter

25g (1oz) flaked almonds

1 garlic clove

1 tsp fresh lemon juice

Salt and pepper

1. Wash and trim the sprouts, place in a pan of boiling water and cook for 5 minutes until just tender. Drain.

2. Melt the butter in a frying pan and add the flaked almonds and crushed garlic. Fry until the almonds are golden brown and stir in the lemon juice. Season with salt and pepper.

3. Add the sprouts to the pan and stir to mix.

Cabbage

As you can grow and pick cabbage all year round it is readily and abundantly available, especially the green varieties.

These 'greens' can often be used as a substitute for spinach (when you have run out of cabbage recipes) but need longer cooking.

The best treatment for a red cabbage is a long, slow casserole with apple and both red and white cabbage can be shredded for salads and stir-fries.

Green Cabbage & Pasta Bake

Serves 4   Preparation 20 minutes   Cooking time 45 minutes

1 small green cabbage

1 medium onion

2 tbsp oil

1 tbsp fresh parsley

350g (12oz) penne pasta

150ml (5fl oz) single cream

50g (2oz) Gruyère cheese

300ml (½ pint) vegetable stock

Salt and pepper

1. Finely shred the cabbage and place in a large bowl.

2. Chop the onion and sauté in hot oil until the onion is transparent. Add to the cabbage. Stir in the chopped parsley.

3. Cook the pasta according to the packet instructions and drain. Mix the pasta with the cabbage and place in a shallow baking dish.

4. Mix the cream with the grated Gruyère and stir in the stock. Season with salt and pepper and pour over the cabbage.

5. Cover and bake at 180ºC (350ºF) Mark 4 for 35 minutes. Remove the cover and allow to brown for the last 5 minutes.

Stir-Fried Green Cabbage

Serves 4   Preparation 20 minutes   Cooking time 10 minutes

500g (1lb) green cabbage

2 medium carrots

1 bunch spring onions

100g (4oz) cashew nuts

2 tbsp oil

2 garlic cloves

2cm (1 inch) piece root ginger

1 dried red chilli

3 tbsp soy sauce

1 tbsp dry sherry

1. Finely shred the cabbage. Cut the carrots into matchsticks and chop the spring onions.

2. Heat the oil and fry the cashew nuts in a large wok on a low heat until brown. Remove from the pan with a slotted spoon.

3. Finely chop the garlic, root ginger and red chilli and add to the pan. Stir and fry for 1 minute. Add the cabbage, carrots and spring onions and continue to stir-fry for 3 minutes.

4. Stir in the soy sauce and sherry and cook for a further 2 minutes. Add the cashew nuts.

5. Serve with rice or noodles.

19

Buttered Cabbage with Sesame Seeds

Serves 4
Preparation 10 minutes
Cooking time 15 minutes

500g (1lb) white cabbage

50g (2oz) butter

1 tbsp sesame seeds

Nutmeg

Salt and pepper

1. Finely shred the cabbage, wash and drain.

2. In a large pan, heat the butter and sauté the cabbage for 15 minutes until softened but still crisp.

3. Stir in the sesame seeds. Season with freshly grated nutmeg and salt and pepper.

White Cabbage in a Creamy Sauce

Serves 4   Preparation 20 minutes   Cooking time 30 minutes

750g (1½lb) white cabbage

Nutmeg

100g (4oz) nuts, e.g. walnuts, peanuts

175g (6oz) cheddar cheese

For the sauce:

75g (3oz) butter

4 tbsp plain flour

600ml (1 pint) milk

Salt and pepper

1. Shred the cabbage and steam until tender. Season well with grated nutmeg.

2. Meanwhile, melt the butter in a pan, stir in the flour and cook for 2 minutes. Gradually add the milk, stirring continuously until the sauce thickens. Season with salt and pepper and simmer gently for 5 minutes.

3. Grease a large baking dish and make alternate layers with cabbage, white sauce, nuts and grated cheese. Bake for 15 minutes on 220°C (425°F) Mark 7.

Red Cabbage Casserole

Serves 4
Preparation 15 minutes
Cooking time 60 minutes

750g (1½lb) red cabbage

2 cooking apples

1 large onion

50g (2oz) raisins

1 tsp sugar

300ml (½ pint) white wine

Salt and pepper

1. Thinly slice the red cabbage, apples and onion and place in a casserole dish.

2. Add the raisins, sugar, salt and pepper and mix well. Stir in the wine. Cover with a lid or foil and bake at 180ºC (350ºF) Mark 4 for 1 hour until the cabbage is tender.

Red Cabbage, Carrot & Watercress Salad

Serves 4   Preparation 15 minutes

½ a small red cabbage

2 carrots

1 bunch watercress

50g (2oz) sesame seeds

For the dressing:

3 tbsp olive oil

2 tbsp fresh lemon juice

1 tbsp honey

Salt and pepper

1. Finely shred the cabbage and mix with the grated carrot. Add the roughly chopped watercress.

2. Dry-fry the sesame seeds in a small frying pan, stirring frequently until lightly browned. Sprinkle on top of the vegetables.

3. Combine the oil, lemon juice and honey in a screw-topped jar and shake to mix. Pour over the salad.

Carrots

All vegetables have a better flavour if grown organically, carrots especially so. Their flavour also depends on how you use them: used raw in salads they are intense and sweet, in soups they are fragrant and mild, and roasted they have a melting sweetness.

Carrots contain large amounts of carotene and vitamin A, along with useful amounts of vitamins B3, C and E. These lie near or in the skin. So, if the carrots are fresh, simply sponge them in running water.

Carrot & Cashew Nut Soup

Serves 6   Preparation 15 minutes   Cooking time 35 minutes

500g (1lb) carrots

250g (8oz) potatoes

1 medium onion

3 tbsp oil

100g (4oz) cashew nuts

2 tsp ground coriander

900ml (1½ pints) vegetable stock

1. Roughly chop the carrots, potatoes and onion and sauté in hot oil until the onion is transparent.

2. Meanwhile, dry-fry the cashew nuts in a small frying pan, stirring frequently, until lightly browned.

3. Add the ground coriander to the vegetable mixture and stir for 2 minutes.

4. Add the stock, bring to the boil, cover and simmer for 25 minutes.

5. Transfer the vegetables to a liquidiser, add the cashew nuts and blend until smooth.

Carrot & Orange Salad

Serves 4   Preparation 15 minutes   Cooking time 10 minutes

500g (1lb) carrots

2 oranges

1 small lettuce

For the dressing:

2cm (1 inch) piece root ginger

3 tbsp red wine vinegar

2 tbsp orange juice

4 tbsp olive oil

2 tbsp poppy seeds

Salt and pepper

1. Cut the carrots into matchsticks and steam for 10 minutes until just tender. Leave to cool.

2. Peel and thinly slice the oranges and mix with finely shredded lettuce and the carrots.

3. Grate the root ginger and combine with the vinegar, orange juice, oil, poppy seeds and seasoning in a screw-topped jar. Shake to mix and pour over salad.

Carrot, Tomato & Ginger Pasta Salad

Serves 4   Preparation 15 minutes   Cooking time 10 minutes

340g (14oz) farfalle pasta

750g (1½lb) carrots

2cm (1 inch) piece root ginger

4 spring onions

4 tomatoes

4 tbsp olive oil

1 tbsp lemon juice

1 tbsp white wine vinegar

1. Cook the pasta. Drain, rinse under cold water and add a little olive oil to prevent sticking.

2. Wash and grate the carrots. Peel and grate the ginger. Finely slice the spring onions and tomatoes. Mix these vegetables together.

3. Combine the oil, lemon juice and vinegar in a screw-topped jar and shake to mix. Pour over the vegetables and mix with the pasta.

Carrot Soufflé with Ginger

Serves 4   Preparation 20 minutes   Cooking time 55 minutes

350g (12oz) carrots

2cm (1 inch) piece root ginger

40g (1½oz) butter

25g (1oz) flour

150ml (5fl oz) of liquid from carrots

3 large eggs

25g (1oz) cheddar cheese

Salt and pepper

1. Wash the carrots and chop into 2cm (1 inch) lengths. Boil until very tender and drain, reserving the cooking liquid.

2. Grate the ginger and add to the carrots. Blend in a liquidiser until smooth, adding a tablespoon of cooking liquid if required.

3. Melt the butter, stir in the flour and cook for 2 minutes. Gradually stir in the reserved cooking liquid and continue stirring until the sauce thickens.

4. Add the carrot mixture and season with salt and pepper.

5. Carefully separate the eggs and beat the egg whites until stiff. Beat the egg yolks and add to the carrot sauce. Gently fold in the egg whites and pour into a greased soufflé dish.

6. Grate the cheese and sprinkle on top. Bake at 200ºC (400ºF) Mark 6 for 30 minutes until set.

Roasted Carrots with Thyme

Serves 4.
Preparation 5 minutes
Cooking time 30 minutes

750g (1½lb) carrots

2 tbsps olive oil

½ tbsp fresh thyme

Salt and pepper

1. Wash the carrots and slice into 1cm (½ inch) slices. Drizzle over the olive oil, stir in the chopped thyme and season with salt and pepper.

2. Roast at 200°C (400°F) Mark 6 for 30 minutes until browned and tender.

Carrot & Tomato Soup

Serves 6   Preparation 15 minutes   Cooking time 35 minutes

500g (1lb) carrots

250g (8oz) potatoes

1 large onion

1 garlic clove

2cm (1 inch) piece root ginger

2 tbsp oil

1 x 400g (14oz) can tomatoes

900ml (1½ pints) vegetable stock

Salt and pepper

1. Roughly chop the carrots, potatoes, onion, garlic and ginger and sauté in hot oil until the onion is transparent.

2. Add the chopped tomatoes and stock. Season with salt and pepper.

3. Bring to the boil, cover and simmer for 25 minutes until tender.

4. Cool slightly, transfer to a liquidiser and blend until smooth. Reheat gently before serving.

Cauliflower

Cauliflower is a vegetable that we tend to overcook making it soggy and grey. So, try it in salads either raw or blanched in boiling water for 2 minutes. You can also add it to a crispy stir-fry - after all, it is thought to have come from China.

Don't throw away all the green leaves, either chop finely and cook along with the florets or use them instead of cabbage in other receipes.

If you find baby cauliflowers you can steam them whole for about 5 minutes and serve as a side vegetable.

Spicy Cauliflower

Serves 4   Preparation 25 minutes   Cooking time 30 minutes

500g (1lb) potatoes

1 medium onion

2 garlic cloves

4 tbsp oil

2cm (1 inch) piece root ginger

1 dried red chilli

1 medium cauliflower

1 tsp ground cumin

1 tsp ground coriander

½ tsp ground turmeric

1 x 400g (14oz) can tomatoes

Salt and pepper

1. Wash the potatoes, chop into 3cm (1½ inch) cubes and boil for 15 minutes until tender. Drain.

2. Slice the onion and sauté in hot oil with the crushed garlic, finely chopped root ginger and chilli until the onion is transparent.

3. Break the cauliflower into small florets and add to the pan. Cook for a few minutes. Stir in the cumin, coriander and turmeric and stir and fry for 2 minutes.

4. Add the chopped tomatoes and 150ml (5fl oz) of water. Bring to a simmer, cover and cook for 10 minutes. Add the potatoes and continue cooking for 5 minutes until the cauliflower is just tender.

Cauliflower & Pea Salad

Serves 4
Preparation 10 minutes
Cooking time 2 minutes

500g (1lb) cauliflower

50g (2oz) fresh peas

450ml (15fl oz) yoghurt

1 tbsp fresh parsley

Salt and pepper

1. Break the cauliflower into small florets and place in a pan of boiling water, along with the peas for 2 minutes. Drain and rinse with cold water.

2. Mix together the yoghurt and chopped parsley and season with salt and pepper. Pour over the cauliflower and refrigerate until cold.

Cauliflower Soup

Serves 6   Preparation time 15 minutes   Cooking time 30 minutes

---

2 tsp cumin seeds

2 tbsp oil

1 medium onion

250g (8oz) potatoes

2 garlic cloves

500g (1lb) cauliflower

900ml (1½ pints) vegetable stock

2 tsp ground turmeric

2 tsp ground cumin

1 tsp ground coriander

4 tbsp fresh coriander

Salt and pepper

1. Roughly chop the onions and potatoes. Heat the oil in a large pan and fry the cumin seeds for a few seconds until they begin to pop. Add the onions, potatoes and the crushed garlic. Sauté until the onion is transparent.

2. Add the ground turmeric, ground cumin and ground coriander, and stir-fry for 2 minutes.

3. Break the cauliflower into florets and roughly chop the leaves. Add to the pan along with the stock. Bring to the boil, cover and simmer for 25 minutes until the cauliflower is tender.

4. Chop the fresh coriander and add to the soup. Transfer to a liquidiser and blend until smooth.

Cauliflower & Sweetcorn Pie

Serves 4   Preparation 30 minutes   Cooking time 45 minutes

1 cauliflower

1 medium onion

1 tbsp oil

25g (1oz) flour

300ml (½ pint) milk

2 tsp mustard

50g (2oz) cheddar cheese

2 tbsp fresh parsley

1 x 200g (6oz) can sweetcorn

Salt and pepper

500g (1lb) pack puff pastry

1 egg yolk

1. Break the cauliflower into florets and steam for 10 minutes until just tender.

2. Chop the onion and sauté in the hot oil for 5 minutes. Add the flour and cook for 1 minute. Gradually stir in the milk and cook until thickened.

3. Stir in the mustard, grated cheese and chopped parsley. Season with salt and pepper.

4. Drain the sweetcorn and add to the pan. Stir in the cauliflower and transfer to a pie dish.

5. Roll out the pastry on a lightly floured surface. Brush the rim of the pie dish with water and cut a strip of pastry to place on the rim.

Brush the pastry rim with water and place the remaining pastry on top. Press the edges together to form a seal and make a hole in the top of the pie to allow steam to escape.

6. Beat the egg yolk and brush over the pie. Bake at 200ºC (400ºF) Mark 6 for 30-35 minutes until golden.

Celeriac

Celeriac is the root of certain types of celery and has a strong celery flavour. It is ugly and knobbly and usually very dirty but tastes delicious (I think).

To use raw you can peel and grate it and smother it with mayonnaise or add it to salads.

To cook celeriac, chop it and boil for 25 minutes, adding a dash of lemon juice to the water. You can serve it mashed with plenty of butter and black pepper.

Celeriac & Blue Cheese Soup

Serves 6   Preparation 15 minutes   Cooking time 40 minutes

500g (1lb) celeriac

1 onion

3 tbsp oil

150ml (5fl oz) dry cider

900ml (1½ pints) vegetable stock

1 cooking apple

150ml (5fl oz) single cream

100g (4oz) blue cheese

Salt and pepper

1. Peel and chop the celeriac and onion. Sauté in hot oil for 10 minutes until the onion is transparent.

2. Add the cider and the stock. Bring to the boil, cover and simmer for 25 minutes until the celeriac is tender.

3. Add the chopped apple and continue to cook for 5 minutes. Transfer to a liquidiser and blend until smooth.

4. Return to the pan. Add the cream and crumbled cheese, heat gently and stir until smooth. Season with salt and pepper.

Fried Celeriac with Cheese

Serves 4   Preparation 15 minutes   Cooking time 20 minutes

500g (1lb) celeriac

2 garlic cloves

3 tbsp oil

2 tbsp fresh parsley

Salt and pepper

50g (2oz) Parmesan cheese

1. Peel the celeriac and cut into matchsticks. Crush the garlic and fry with the celeriac for 15 minutes, stirring frequently.

2. Stir in the finely chopped parsley and season with salt and pepper. Transfer to a shallow dish.

3. Grate the cheese and sprinkle on top of the celeriac mixture. Place under a hot grill until the cheese is melted and brown.

Roasted Celeriac

Serves 4
Preparation 15 minutes
Cooking time 40 minutes

750g (1½lb celeriac)

2 garlic cloves

1 tbsp fresh thyme leaves

3 tbsp olive oil

Salt and pepper

1. Peel the celeriac, chop into 2cm (1 inch) chunks and place in a large roasting tray.

2. Add the crushed garlic, thyme and oil. Season with salt and pepper. Stir well to mix. Roast at 200ºC (400ºF) Mark 6 for 30-40 minutes.

Celery

When you eat a stick of celery you use up more calories than it contains because it needs so much chewing. But not if you've filled it with cream cheese or dipped it in something tasty, which is one of the best things to do with it.

Use raw in salads and stir-fries for an extra crunch. Celery soup has a distinctive sharp flavour and you can add the leaves as well.

If your celery has gone a bit limp, revive it by wrapping in kitchen roll and standing it in a jar of water.

Celery Soup

Serves 6   Preparation 15 minutes   Cooking time 35 minutes

1 head of celery

2 medium potatoes

1 large onion

2 tbsp oil

100g (4oz) cashew nuts

900ml (1½ pints) vegetable stock

300ml (½ pint) milk

Salt and pepper

1. Roughly chop the celery, potatoes and onion and sauté in hot oil until the onion is transparent.

2. Stir in the cashew nuts and continue to cook for 5 minutes, stirring frequently.

3. Add the stock and bring to the boil. Cover and simmer for 25 minutes until the vegetables are tender.

4. Cool slightly, transfer to a liquidiser and blend until smooth. Stir in the milk and season to taste. Reheat before serving.

Celery & Walnut Salad

Serves 4
Preparation 15 minutes

1 head of celery

1 bunch of watercress

200ml (7fl oz) natural yoghurt

3 tbsp olive oil

1 tbsp lemon juice

100g (4oz) chopped walnuts

Salt and pepper

1. Wash the celery and watercress. Chop and place in a serving bowl.

2. Mix together the yoghurt, olive oil and lemon juice until smooth. Add the chopped walnuts and season with salt and pepper.

3. Spoon the dressing over the salad and refrigerate before serving.

Celery & Mushroom Pasta Sauce

Serves 4   Preparation 20 minutes   Cooking time 25 minutes

1 head of celery

1 medium onion

4 tbsp olive oil

150g (6oz) mushrooms

25g (1oz) flour

150ml (5fl oz) vegetable stock

150ml (5fl oz) single cream

Salt and pepper

1. Finely chop the celery and slice the onion. Heat the oil and add the vegetables. Cover and cook for 15 minutes.

2. Slice the mushrooms, add to the pan and cook for a further 5 minutes.

3. Stir in the flour and cook for 1 minute. Gradually add the stock and stir until the sauce thickens. Stir in the cream and season with salt and pepper.

4. Serve with freshly cooked fusilli.

Courgettes

You can grow courgettes very easily and the more you pick them the more the plants produce (which is why I have included so many recipes). They are basically immature marrows but, unless squashy, limp and pithy, they taste much better. Bright yellow courgettes add colour and you can use them as you would the green varieties.

Slice thinly for salads or a stir-fry. If you overcook them they go soggy so catch them when they are just crisp. Fry for 5-10 minutes, or roast in a very hot oven with olive oil and fresh basil.

Courgette, Tomato & Feta Pasta Sauce

Serves 4   Preparation 20 minutes   Cooking time 20 minutes

1 large onion

2 garlic cloves

2 tbsp olive oil

3 large courgettes

3 large tomatoes

200g (7oz) feta cheese

3 tbsp fresh mint

Salt and pepper

1. Slice the onion, crush the garlic and sauté in hot oil until the onion is transparent.

2. Wash the courgettes, halve them lengthways and cut into 1cm (½ inch) chunks. Add the courgettes to the pan and cook for 5 minutes, stirring occasionally. Now add the chopped tomatoes and cook for 2 minutes.

3. Remove the pan from the heat. Chop the feta cheese into cubes and add to the pan. Season with salt and pepper. Stir in the chopped mint.

4. Serve with freshly cooked penne.

Courgette Tart

For the shortcrust pastry:

175g (6oz) plain flour

Pinch of salt

75g (3oz) margarine

2 tbsp cold water

For the filling:

750g (1½lb) courgettes

2 tbsp oil

1 tbsp fresh thyme leaves

4 garlic cloves

4 eggs

300ml (½ pint) milk

Salt and pepper

1. Sift the flour and salt into a bowl. Cut the margarine into small pieces and rub into the flour until the mixture resembles fine breadcrumbs. Add 2 tablespoons of cold water to mix to a firm dough, then wrap in cling film and chill for 30 minutes.

2. Meanwhile, to prepare the filling, slice the courgettes into ½cm (¼ inch) chunks and sauté gently in hot oil for 10 minutes until softened. Add the chopped thyme, season well and leave to cool.

3. Put the garlic cloves in a small pan of boiling water and blanch until soft. Peel and mash well with a fork.

4. Roll out the pastry on a lightly floured surface to line a 20cm (8 inch) flan dish. Prick entire surface with a fork and bake blind at 200ºC (400ºF) Mark 6 for 15 minutes until just firm to the touch.

5. Beat the eggs and milk together and add the mashed garlic. Spread the courgettes into the pastry case and pour over the egg and milk mixture.

6. Bake at 200ºC (400ºF) Mark 6 for 20 minutes until set.

Courgette & Aubergine Couscous

Serves 4   Preparation 25 minutes   Cooking time 40 minutes

2 large courgettes

1 aubergine

250g (8oz) tomatoes

1 large onion

2 red or yellow peppers

2 garlic cloves

4 tbsp olive oil

280g (10oz) couscous

600ml (1 pint) vegetable stock

1 lettuce

For the dressing:

4 tbsp olive oil

2 tbsp white wine vinegar

1 tbsp ground cumin

1 tbsp tomato purée

Salt and pepper

1. Chop the courgettes, aubergine, tomatoes, onion and peppers into 2cm (1 inch) chunks. Finely chop the garlic. Place all the vegetables in a large roasting tray.

2. Mix in the oil and stir well to give a good coating. Roast at 200ºC (400ºF) Mark 6 for 40 minutes, stirring half way through. Leave to cool.

3. Place the couscous in a large bowl and pour on the stock. When all the stock is absorbed stir gently with a fork. Leave to cool.

4. To make the dressing combine all the ingredients in a screw-topped jar and shake vigorously.

5. Mix the roasted vegetables with the couscous. Pour over the dressing and serve with shredded lettuce.

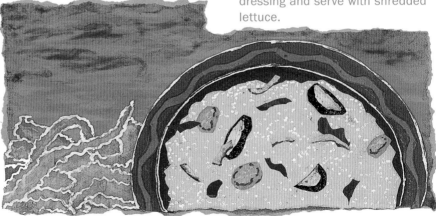

Courgette Soup

Serves 6   Preparation 15 minutes   Cooking time 30 minutes

3 medium potatoes

2 medium onions

2 sticks of celery

2 tbsp oil

4 medium courgettes

900ml (1½ pints) vegetable stock

75g (3oz) cheddar cheese

Salt and pepper

1. Wash and chop potatoes. Cut the onions and celery into large chunks and sauté with the potatoes in hot oil until the onion is transparent.

2. Cut the courgettes into 2cm (1 inch) slices and add to the pan along with the vegetable stock.

3. Bring to the boil, cover and simmer for 20 minutes, until tender.

4. Transfer to a liquidiser and blend until smooth. Add the grated cheese, salt and pepper and reheat gently before serving.

Courgette & Basil Pasta Sauce

Serves 4   Preparation 15 minutes   Cooking time 25 minutes

1kg (2lb) courgettes

2 garlic cloves

3 tbsp olive oil

2 tbsp fresh basil

150ml (5fl oz) double cream

Salt and pepper

1. Slice the courgettes into 1cm (½ inch) pieces and fry gently with the crushed garlic for 20 minutes until brown. Add 2 tablespoons of water and stir well.

2. Chop the basil and add to the pan. Stir in the double cream and cook gently to heat through. Season with salt and pepper.

3. Serve with freshly cooked fusilli.

Stir-Fried Courgettes

Serves 4
Preparation 10 minutes
Cooking time 3 minutes

500g (1lb) courgettes

2 tbsp olive oil

2 garlic cloves

1 tbsp dry sherry

1. Cut the courgettes into matchsticks.

2. Crush the garlic and fry in hot oil for a few seconds. Add the courgettes and stir-fry for 3 minutes.

3. Stir in the sherry and serve.

Courgette & Tomato Pie

Serves 4   Preparation 20 minutes   Cooking time 55 minutes

For the topping:

750g (1½lb) potatoes

25g (1oz) butter

4 tbsp milk

4 spring onions

For the filling:

4 courgettes

2 medium onions

2 garlic cloves

6 tomatoes

1 tbsp tomato purée

Salt and pepper

1. Chop the potatoes and cook in boiling water for 20 minutes until tender. Drain and mash with the butter and the milk. Stir in the chopped spring onions.

2. Meanwhile, slice the courgettes into 1cm (½ inch) pieces and finely slice the onions. Sauté together in hot oil for 10 minutes. Add the crushed garlic, chopped tomatoes and tomato puree. Season with salt and pepper, cover and simmer for 5 minutes.

3. Place the courgette mixture into an ovenproof dish and spoon the mashed potato on top. Bake at 190ºC (375ºF) Mark 5 for 30 minutes.

Cucumber

Apparently the indigestibility has been bred out of cucumbers and you can even grow a variety called Burpless Tasty Green - which is a good description of a cucumber. You can now grow them outdoors, without glass, and watch them scramble along the ground.

Cucumbers, a thing of beauty, smooth-skinned and a full 12 inches, are best served raw in salads. Or cut them very thinly for a posh summer sandwich. A glut of cucumbers calls for a soup which you can serve hot or ice cold.

Cucumber & Tomato Couscous

Serves 6   Preparation 10 minutes

280g (10oz) couscous

5 tbsp olive oil

1 lemon

1 cucumber

280g (10oz) tomatoes

1 bunch spring onions

2 tbsp fresh mint

2 tbsp fresh parsley

Salt and pepper

1. Cover the couscous with boiling water and leave to stand for 5 minutes. Fluff up with a fork and stir in the olive oil and juice from the lemon. Season with salt and pepper.

2. Cut the cucumber in half lengthways and slice thinly. Chop the tomatoes and spring onions. Add the vegetables to the couscous.

3. Finely chop the mint and parsley and stir into the salad. Refrigerate until chilled.

Cucumber Relish

Serves 4
Preparation 10 minutes

½ a cucumber

4 spring onions

2 medium tomatoes

½ tsp cayenne pepper

1 tbsp lemon juice

Salt

1. Peel and dice the cucumber. Mix with the finely chopped spring onions.

2. Peel the tomatoes, cut in half, discard the seeds and dice.

3. Mix the tomatoes and the remaining ingredients with the cucumber.

Cucumber & Watercress Soup

Serves 6   Preparation 15 minutes   Cooking time 40 minutes

1 medium onion

2 tbsp oil

1 tsp ground cumin

1 tsp ground coriander

250g (8oz) potatoes

1 cucumber

600ml (1 pint) vegetable stock

1 bunch of watercress

300ml (½ pint) milk

Salt and pepper

1. Roughly chop the onion and sauté in hot oil until the onion is transparent. Stir in the cumin and coriander and fry for 2 minutes.

2. Wash and chop the potatoes and cucumber and add to the pan along with the stock. Bring to the boil, cover and simmer for 20 minutes.

3. Chop the watercress and add to the pan. Season with salt and pepper and simmer for a further 10 minutes.

4. Stir in the milk, transfer to a liquidiser and blend until smooth. Reheat before serving, or serve cold.

Cucumber & Apple Salad

Serves 4   Preparation 15 minutes

1 cucumber

2 apples

1 tsp lemon juice

½ tbsp fresh dill

½ tbsp fresh chives

For the dressing:

4 tbsp olive oil

2 tbsp white wine vinegar

1 tbsp yoghurt

Salt and pepper

1. Finely slice the cucumber. Cut the apple into quarters, remove the core and slice thinly. Stir the lemon juice into the apple to prevent discolouring.

2. To make the dressing, combine the oil, vinegar, yoghurt and seasoning in a screw-topped jar and shake vigorously.

3. Mix together the cucumber and apple. Finely chop the dill and chives and sprinkle over the salad. Pour the dressing on top.

41

Fennel

Fennel has a distinct taste of aniseed which you either love or hate. This flavour goes very well with fish, so you could serve Fennel & Potato Gratin as an accompaniment.

I also like to serve it as a main vegetarian course with Roasted Carrots with Thyme.

When you use fennel raw in salads remove the first layer of skin if it is tough. Slice the fennel thinly. Use the feathery leaves in salads or as a garnish.

Fennel & Potato Gratin

Serves 6   Preparation 25 minutes   Cooking time 50 minutes

2 fennel bulbs

600ml (1 pint) vegetable stock

1kg (2lb) potatoes

1 large onion

1 tbsp oil

450ml (¾ pint) milk

50g (2oz) cheddar cheese

1. Thinly slice the fennel. Place in a pan with the stock, cover and simmer for 10-15 minutes until just tender. Drain.

2. Slice the potatoes into 1cm (½ inch) pieces and boil for 5 minutes until tender.

3. Thinly slice the onion and sauté in hot oil until the onion is transparent.

4. Mix the fennel, potatoes and onion together and place in a shallow baking dish. Pour the milk over the vegetables and sprinkle the cheese on top. Bake at 180°C (350°F) Mark 4 for 40 minutes.

Fennel Soup

Serves 6
Preparation 15 minutes
Cooking time 40 minutes

3 fennel bulbs

250g (8oz) potatoes

1 small onion

900ml (1½ pints) vegetable stock

2 stems lemon grass

150ml (5fl oz) double cream

Salt and pepper

1. Roughly chop the fennel, potatoes and onion. Add to the stock with the lemon grass. Bring to the boil, cover and simmer for 35 minutes.

2. Remove the lemon grass, stir in the cream and season with salt and pepper. Transfer to a liquidiser and blend until smooth. Reheat gently before serving.

Fennel Couscous

Serves 4   Preparation 15 minutes

250g (8oz) couscous

2 tbsp olive oil

2 tbsp white wine vinegar

1 lemon

1 fennel bulb

1 bunch spring onions

2 tbsp fresh parsley

2 tbsp fresh mint

Salt and pepper

1. Cover the couscous with boiling water and leave to stand for 5 minutes.

2. Fluff up the couscous with a fork and stir in the olive oil, white wine vinegar and the juice from the lemon. Season with salt and pepper.

3. Finely slice the fennel and spring onions and add to the couscous.

4. Chop the parsley and mint and add to the salad. Mix well and refrigerate until chilled.

Green Beans

Although green beans have been cultivated for thousands of years, the runner bean was only grown as an ornamental flower, not as a vegetable until late Victorian times.

For these recipes you can use the French beans (Haricot Vert) or runner beans. The runner bean is our favourite for home growing in the UK. It is quite easy to grow and provides masses of beans.

To prepare runner beans you should top and tail them and pull off the stringy edges.

Green Bean & Tomato Salad

Serves 4   Preparation 15 minutes   Cooking time 10 minutes

500g (1lb) green beans

1kg (2lb) tomatoes

1 bunch spring onions

1 tbsp fresh tarragon

For the dressing:

3 tbsp olive oil

1 tbsp white wine vinegar

1 tbsp lemon juice

Salt and pepper

1. Steam the beans for 10-15 minutes until just tender. Leave to cool.

2. Chop the tomatoes into quarters and finely slice the spring onions. Mix with the beans and chopped tarragon.

3. Combine the oil, vinegar, lemon juice, salt and pepper in a screw-topped jar and shake to mix. Pour over the salad.

Green Beans with Almonds

Serves 4
Preparation 15 minutes
Cooking time 10 minutes

500g (1lb) green beans

2 tbsp oil

50g (2oz) flaked almonds

Salt and pepper

1. Top and tail and finely slice the green beans. Steam them for 10-15 minutes until tender.

2. Fry the almonds in hot oil until browned, remove from the pan and drain on kitchen paper.

3. Put the beans into the frying pan, cover and cook gently for a further 3 minutes. Stir in the almonds and season with salt and pepper.

Spicy Green Beans

Serves 4   Preparation 15 minutes   Cooking time 30 minutes

750g (1½lb) green beans

4cm (2 inch) piece root ginger

1 garlic clove

6 tbsp oil

½ tsp ground turmeric

1 tsp ground cumin

2 tsp ground coriander

3 tbsp fresh coriander

1. Wash and trim the beans and cut into 6cm (3 inch) lengths.

2. Pccl and finely chop the root ginger and garlic and fry in hot oil for 2 minutes. Add the turmeric, cumin and coriander and cook stirring for 1 minute.

3. Add the green beans and the chopped fresh coriander. Stir in 3 tablespoons of water and season with salt. Cover the pan and cook on a low heat for 25-30 minutes.

Jerusalem Artichokes

Jerusalem artichokes are not a popular vegetable, despite their grow-anywhere hardiness. This may be because they make you fart, they are very knobbly and have a strong, some would say unpleasant taste.

To blunt their flavour you can mix them with potatoes and mash with plenty of butter. However, if you are a fan then try this soufflé and soup.

You can cook Jerusalem artichokes as you would potatoes, so fry them or add them to a mixed roasted vegetable dish.

Jerusalem Artichoke Soufflé

Serves 4   Preparation 30 minutes   Cooking time 50 minutes

350g (12oz) Jerusalem artichokes

100g (4oz) celery

½ a lemon

4 large eggs

For the white sauce:

75g (2½ oz) margarine

40g (1½ oz) flour

200ml (7 fl oz) milk

50g (2oz) Parmesan cheese

1 garlic clove

1 tsp paprika

Salt

1. Wash the artichokes and chop into 1cm (½ inch) chunks. Steam with the chopped celery for 20 minutes until soft. Transfer to a liquidiser, add the juice from the lemon, and blend until smooth.

2. Melt the margarine, add the flour and cook, stirring for 1 minute. Slowly add the milk and continue stirring until the sauce thickens. Stir in the grated Parmesan, crushed garlic, paprika and salt.

3. Separate the eggs. Stir the yolks into the artichoke mixture and mix into the white sauce. Beat the egg whites until stiff and fold into the artichoke mixture.

4. Grease a large soufflé dish, pour in the soufflé mixture and bake at 200°C (400°F) Mark 6 for 25 minutes. Serve immediately.

Jerusalem Artichoke Mash

Serves 4
Preparation 10 minutes
Cooking time 20 minutes

500g (1lb) Jerusalem
artichokes

500g (1lb) potatoes

100g (4oz) butter

50g (2oz) cheddar cheese

Salt and pepper

1. Wash the artichokes and potatoes
   and cut into even sized pieces.
   Place into a pan of boiling water
   and cook for 15-20 minutes until
   tender. Drain.

2. Mash with a potato masher and
   mix in the butter and cheese.
   Season with salt and pepper.

Jerusalem Artichoke Soup

Serves 6   Preparation 20 minutes   Cooking time 30 minutes

500g (1lb) Jerusalem
artichokes

1 medium onion

2 tbsp oil

900ml (1½ pints) vegetable
stock

150ml (5fl oz) milk

50g (2oz) cheddar cheese

Salt and pepper

1. Wash and thinly slice the
   artichokes.

2. Chop the onion and sauté in hot
   oil until the onion is transparent.
   Add the artichokes and stock.
   Bring to the boil, cover and
   simmer for 20 minutes until the
   artichokes are tender. Season with
   salt and pepper.

3. Transfer to a liquidiser and blend
   until smooth. Stir in the cream.
   Return to the pan, stir in the
   cheese and reheat gently before
   serving.

Kohlrabi

Kohlrabi is a bit like a turnip and a bit like a cabbage and, like them, belongs to the brassica family. Although we usually associate brassicas with greens, not all of them are leafy vegetables.

The kohlrabi globe has a slightly nutty flavour and is delicious grated raw in salads. You can cook the leaves as you would spinach.

If you grow your own, lift when the globes are undersized, cook whole and serve with a cheese sauce. With larger ones, slice and cook long and slow as in this gratin.

Kohlrabi Gratin

Serves 4   Preparation 20 minutes   Cooking time 60 minutes

1kg (2lb) kohlrabi

3 tbsp fresh parsley

1 lemon

50g (2oz) butter

300ml (½ pint) single cream

100g (4oz) Cheddar cheese

Salt and pepper

1. Peel the kohlrabi, cut in half and slice thinly. Place half in a gratin dish and sprinkle with half the chopped parsley.

2. Finely grate the lemon rind and sprinkle half on top of the kohlrabi. Dot over half of the butter. Season with salt and pepper.

3. Put the remaining kohlrabi, parsley and lemon rind on top. Dot with the remaining butter and pour over the cream.

4. Top with the grated cheese and bake at 190°C (375°F) Mark 5 for 60 minutes until tender.

Kohlrabi Salad

Serves 4
Preparation 15 minutes

1 medium kohlrabi

2 carrots

1 apple

Juice of 1 lemon

100g (4oz) peanuts

3 tbsp mustard seeds

3 tbsp olive oil

1. Peel and grate the kohlrabi. Wash
   and grate the carrots and apple.
   Mix with the lemon juice and add
   the peanuts.

2. Fry the mustard seeds in the hot
   oil until they begin to pop. Pour
   the seeds and oil over the salad
   and mix well. Serve cold.

Kohlrabi & Fennel Soup

Serves 6   preparation 15 minutes   Cooking time 35 minutes

2 medium kohlrabi

1 fennel bulb

1 large onion

2 tbsp oil

900ml (1½ pints) vegetable
stock

300ml (½ pint) milk

Salt and pepper

1. Slice the kohlrabi, fennel and
   onion and sauté in hot oil for
   10 minutes, stirring occasionally.

2. Pour in the stock and season with
   salt and pepper. Bring to the boil,
   cover and simmer for 25 minutes
   until the vegetables are tender.

3. Transfer to a liquidiser and blend
   until smooth. Add the milk and
   reheat gently before serving.

Leeks

Leeks have been enjoyed by our ancestors from the Dark Ages onwards, but I wonder if they enjoyed that cold leek soup 'Crème Vichyssoise'. If you like it hot (and I do) try this traditional leek and potato soup recipe.

The best way to clean a leek is to trim the ends, slit down the length and wash under running water.

You can slice raw leeks finely for a salad. Better still, add them to a stir-fry or wrap them in light puff pastry for this filling pie.

Leek Pie

Serves 6   Preparation 30 minutes   Cooking time 35 minutes

500g (1lb) leeks

2 tbsp oil

3 tbsp cream or yoghurt

2 tsp mustard

2 tsp fresh thyme

1 tsp grated nutmeg

500g (1lb) pack puff pastry

1 egg

Salt and pepper

1. Slice the leeks and sauté in hot oil for 10 minutes until just tender. Season with salt and pepper.

2. Meanwhile, divide the pastry into two and roll into 25cm (10 inch) circles.

3. Mix together the cream, mustard, chopped thyme and grated nutmeg, and add to the leeks.

4. Heap the leek mixture in the centre of one pastry circle leaving a 1cm (½ inch) space around the edge. Brush the edge with water and place the other pastry circle on the top. Press firmly together and make vertical cuts along the two edges with a sharp knife.

5. Brush the pie with the beaten egg yolk. Bake at 220ºC (425ºF) Mark 7 for 35 minutes until risen and golden brown.

Leek & Potato Soup

Serves 6   Preparation 20 minutes   Cooking time 30 minutes

500g (1lb) leeks

250g (8oz) potatoes

1 medium onion

4 tbsp oil

900ml (1½ pints) vegetable stock

300ml (½ pint) milk

Salt and pepper

1. Slice the leeks and roughly chop the potatoes and onion. Sauté the vegetables in hot oil for 10 minutes.

2. Add the stock and season with salt and pepper. Bring to the boil, cover and simmer for 20 minutes until vegetables are tender.

3. Stir in the milk. Transfer to a liquidiser and blend until smooth. Reheat gently before serving.

Creamy Leek Quiche

Serves 6   Preparation 30 minutes   Cooking time 45 minutes

For the shortcrust pastry:

175g (6oz) plain flour

Pinch of salt

75g (3oz) margarine

2 tbsp cold water

For the filling:

750g (1½lb) leeks

2 tbsp oil

3 eggs

150ml (5fl oz) milk

100g (4oz) cheddar cheese

¼ tsp grated nutmeg

Salt and pepper

1. Sift the flour and salt into a bowl. Cut the margarine into small pieces and rub into the flour until the mixture resembles fine breadcrumbs. Add 2 tablespoons of cold water to mix to a firm dough, then wrap in cling film and chill for 30 minutes.

2. Meanwhile, to prepare the filling, slice the leeks and sauté gently in hot oil for 15 minutes until softened. Season well and leave to cool.

3. Roll out the pastry on a lightly floured surface to line a 20cm (8 inch) flan dish. Prick the entire surface with a fork and bake blind at 200ºC (400ºF) Mark 6 for 15 minutes until just firm to the touch.

4. Beat the eggs and milk together and add the grated nutmeg. Sprinkle half of the grated cheese into the pastry case. Spread the leeks on top, pour over the egg and milk mixture and sprinkle the remaining cheese on top.

5. Bake at 200ºC (400ºF) Mark 6 for 30-40 minutes until set and browned.

Lettuce

There are many different varieties of lettuce and they must all be eaten fresh. If left to grow for too long, the heart will begin to grow upwards and your lettuce will bolt. So, grow quickly and pick early.

Once considered a powerful aphrodisiac, lettuce has since been found to contain opium-like substances. But don't smoke it when you have the inevitable summer glut - try lettuce soup.

Try adding a variety of fresh herbs or toasted seeds to salads. Pour over the dressing just before serving.

Chilled Lettuce & Watercress Soup

Serves 6   Preparation 10 minutes   Cooking time 20 minutes

250g (8oz) potatoes

1 bunch spring onions

600ml (1 pint) vegetable stock

2 little gem lettuces

300ml (½ pint) milk

1 bunch watercress

Salt and pepper

1. Roughly chop the potatoes and spring onions. Simmer in the stock for 10 minutes.

2. Shred the lettuce, add to the pan and continue to simmer for a further 10 minutes until the vegetables are tender. Season with salt and pepper.

3. Add the milk. Transfer to a liquidiser and blend until smooth. Stir in the roughly chopped watercress, and blend for a few seconds.

4. Serve chilled or hot.

Seeded Green Salad

Serves 4   Preparation 15 minutes

Mixed lettuce leaves

1 tbsp fresh parsley

½ tbsp pumpkin seeds

½ tbsp sunflower seeds

½ tbsp sesame seeds

For the dressing:

2 tbsp white wine vinegar

6 tbsp olive oil

1 tsp mustard

Pinch of sugar

Salt and pepper

1. Wash and shred the lettuce and put into a bowl. Add the finely chopped parsley.

2. Dry-fry all of the seeds in a small frying pan until browned and popping. Leave to cool and mix into the salad.

3. Combine the ingredients for the dressing in a screw-topped jar and shake to mix. Pour over the salad.

Lettuce with Peas

Serves 4   Preparation 15 minutes   Cooking time 20 minutes

1 small lettuce

1 bunch spring onions

500g (1lb) shelled fresh peas

1 tsp sugar

Salt and pepper

2 tbsp fresh mint

1. Shred the lettuce and chop the spring onions. Combine the lettuce, peas, spring onions and sugar in a saucepan. Season with salt and pepper.

2. Add 150ml (5fl oz) of water and simmer for 20 minutes until the peas are tender. Stir in the chopped mint.

Mushrooms

You should never wash a mushroom: simply wipe with a damp cloth if necessary and trim only the very end off the stems. As they soak up a lot of fat during cooking it is best to use olive oil or butter for frying.

Button mushrooms are ideal for eating raw in salads - particularly if you can eat them within hours of picking.

These recipes use mushrooms as a main ingredient to give a strong mushroomy flavour, especially if you use the darker, brown coloured chestnut variety.

Mushroom & Courgette Pasta Sauce

Serves 4   Preparation 20 minutes   Cooking time 30 minutes

3 medium courgettes

3 tbsp olive oil

280g (10oz) mushrooms

1 medium onion

2 garlic cloves

150ml (5fl oz) white wine

150ml (5fl oz) double cream

1 tbsp fresh tarragon

Salt and pepper

1. Wash the courgettes, cut in half lengthways and slice into ½ cm (¼ inch) chunks. Sauté in 2 tablespoons of hot oil for 5 minutes until just tender. Remove with a slotted spoon and set aside.

2. Add an extra tablespoon of oil to the pan. Slice the mushrooms and onion, chop the garlic and sauté together for 10 minutes. Add the wine and cook gently for 10 minutes.

3. Add the courgettes to the mushroom mixture and stir in the cream. Season with salt and pepper and simmer for a few minutes. Stir in the chopped tarragon.

4. Serve with freshly cooked tagliatelle.

Mushroom Salad

Serves 4
Preparation 10 minutes

750g (1½lb) mushrooms

100g (4oz) Parmesan cheese

2 tbsp lemon juice

5 tbsp olive oil

Salt and pepper

1. Wipe the mushrooms with a damp
   cloth and slice finely.

2. Shave the Parmesan into thin
   wafers and scatter on top of the
   mushrooms.

3. Combine the lemon juice, olive oil,
   salt and pepper in a screw-topped
   jar and shake vigorously to mix.
   Pour over the salad.

Mushrooms with Onion & Ginger

Serves 4   Preparation 15 minutes   Cooking time 20 minutes

1 medium onion

4 tbsp oil

3 garlic cloves

2cm (1 inch) piece root ginger

½ tsp ground turmeric

¼ tsp chilli powder

350g (12oz) mushrooms

Salt and pepper

1. Finely chop the onion and fry in
   hot oil for 5 minutes until lightly
   browned. Add the crushed garlic
   and fincly choppcd gingcr. Fry for
   a further 2 minutes. Add the
   turmeric and chilli powder and stir
   for a few seconds.

2. Cut the mushrooms into quarters
   and add to the onion mixture. Stir
   for 1 minute and add 150ml
   (6fl oz) of water. Season with salt
   and pepper, cover the pan and
   simmer gently for 10 minutes.

Mushroom & Leek Pie

Serves 6   Preparation 25 minutes   Cooking time 60 minutes

500g (1lb) leeks

500g (1lb) mushrooms

4 tbsp oil

25g (1oz) flour

150ml (5fl oz) white wine

150ml (5fl oz) vegetable stock

150ml (5fl oz) double cream

3 tbsp fresh parsley

100g (4oz) Cheddar cheese

500g (1lb) pack puff pastry

1 egg yolk

Salt and pepper

1. Wash and thickly slice the leeks and sauté in hot oil for 10 minutes until tender. Add the sliced mushrooms and cook for a further 10 minutes until the juices have evaporated.

2. Stir in the flour, cook for 1 minute and gradually add the wine and stock. Cook until thickened and stir in the cream.

3. Stir in the chopped parsley and grated cheese and season with salt and pepper. Transfer to a pie dish.

4. Roll out the pastry on a floured surface and cut a thin strip to place on the rim of the pie dish. Brush this pastry rim with water. Place the remaining pastry on top and press down firmly. Make a small hole in the centre for the steam to escape.

5. Brush the top with beaten egg yolk and bake at 200ºC (400ºF) Mark 6 for 40 minutes until the pastry is golden brown.

59

Onions

Onions, one of our oldest vegetables, have been eaten for thousands of years. They are quick and easy to grow from bulbs.

If you get your vegetables through an organic box scheme you always have onions. Apart from using them as a basic ingredient in many recipes they are delicious in their own right. Try this classic onion tart and discover their soft, sweet flavour.

If you cry when chopping onions try breathing through your mouth: not particularly attractive but it works for me.

Onion Tart

Serves 6   Preparation 30 minutes   Cooking time 60 minutes

For the shortcrust pastry:

175g (6oz) plain flour

Pinch of salt

75g (3oz) margarine

2 tbsp cold water

For the filling:

1kg (2lb) onions

3 tbsp oil

2 garlic cloves

2 tbsp white wine

2 eggs

150ml (5fl oz) milk

Salt and pepper

1. Sift the flour and salt into a bowl. Cut the margarine into small pieces and rub into the flour until the mixture resembles fine breadcrumbs. Add 2 tablespoons of cold water to mix to a firm dough, then wrap in cling film and chill for 30 minutes.

2. Meanwhile, thinly slice the onions and garlic and sauté gently in hot oil for 30 minutes until browned. Add the white wine and cook for 5 minutes, stirring frequently.

3. Roll out the pastry to line a 20cm (8 inch) flan dish. Bake blind at 200°C (400°F) Mark 6 for 15 minutes until firm to the touch.

4. Put the onion mixture into the pastry case. Combine the beaten eggs with the milk, salt and pepper and pour over the onion mixture. Bake at 200°C (400°F) Mark 6 for 30 minutes until set and golden.

Onion & Mustard Sauce

Serves 4
Preparation 10 minutes
Cooking time 40 minutes

350g (12oz) onions

75g (3oz) butter

200ml (7fl oz) vegetable stock

1 tbsp mustard

1 tsp sugar

Salt and pepper

1. Finely slice the onions. Melt the butter in a frying pan, add the onions, cover and cook for 25 minutes. Remove the lid and continue cooking for 5 minutes until the liquid has evaporated.

2. Add the stock, mustard and sugar and season with salt and pepper. Simmer for 10 minutes until the sauce is thick and syrupy.

Roasted Onion & Garlic Soup

Serves 6   Preparation 15 minutes   Cooking time 45 minutes

1kg (2lb) onions

6 garlic cloves

3 tbsp oil

900ml (1½ pints) vegetable stock

2 tbsp sherry

Salt and pepper

1. Peel the onions and cut into quarters. Peel the garlic cloves. Mix the onions and garlic with the oil and place in a roasting tray. Roast at 190°C (375°F) Mark 5 for 40 minutes until tender and golden brown.

2. Add the stock and transfer to a liquidiser. Blend until smooth.

3. Place in a pan and season with salt and pepper. Add the sherry and reheat before serving.

Onion & Potato Tart

Serves 6   Preparation 30 minutes   Cooking time 40 minutes

For the shortcrust pastry:

175g (6oz) plain flour

Pinch of salt

75g (3oz) margarine

2 tbsp cold water

For the filling:

250g (8oz) potatoes

250g (8oz) onions

1 tbsp fresh thyme

2 tbsp oil

2 tbsp pesto sauce

50g (2oz) Cheddar cheese

1. Sift the flour and salt into a bowl. Cut the margarine into small pieces and rub into the flour until the mixture resembles fine breadcrumbs. Add 2 tablespoons of cold water to mix to a firm dough, then wrap in cling film and chill for 30 minutes.

2. Meanwhile, cut the potatoes into 1cm (½ inch) slices and cook in boiling water for 10 minutes until just tender. Drain.

3. Chop the thyme, slice the onions and sauté together in hot oil for 15 minutes until the onions are lightly browned.

4. Roll out the pastry on a lightly floured surface to line a 20cm (8 inch) flan dish. Prick the entire surface with a fork and bake blind at 200°C (400°F) Mark 6 for 15 minutes until just firm to the touch.

5. Spread the pesto sauce over the base of the pastry case. Arrange the potatoes on top and then add the onion mixture. Sprinkle the grated cheese over the tart and bake at 200°C (400°F) Mark 6 for 20 minutes.

Caramelised Onion Pasta Sauce

Serves 4   Preparation 15 minutes   Cooking time 60 minutes

750g (1½lb) onions

3 tbsp oil

1 tbsp brown sugar

1 tbsp fresh thyme

150ml (5fl oz) white wine

3 tbsp white wine vinegar

Salt and pepper

50g (2oz) Parmesan cheese

1. Peel and finely slice the onions. Sauté in hot oil for 15 minutes until lightly browned. Season with salt and pepper. Stir in the sugar, cover and cook for 2 minutes until the sugar is caramelised.

2. Stir in the white wine, the vinegar and chopped thyme. Simmer, without the lid, for 45 minutes until the onions are soft.

3. Serve with freshly cooked tagliatelle and grated Parmesan.

Parsnips

Before the introduction of potatoes, parsnips were our main everyday vegetable. But parsnip popularity has been in decline since its heyday during the Dark Ages (5th - 10th centuries).

Parsnips have a strong, sweet flavour and have traditionally been used for jams, puddings and parsnip wine. Cooking them with apples brings out their sweetness and makes this delicious soup.

You can boil them, but why bother when they taste so much better roasted in oil for 40 minutes in a hot oven.

Parsnip & Potato Dauphinois

Serves 4   Preparation 25 minutes   Cooking time 60 minutes

500g (1lb) parsnips

1kg (2lb) potatoes

1 medium onion

2 garlic cloves

50g (2oz) butter

100g (4oz) butter

50g (2oz) cheddar cheese

300ml (½ pint) single cream

Salt and pepper

1. Thinly slice the parsnips, potatoes and onion (use the slicing blade of a food processor if available). Finely chop the garlic.

2. Put a layer of parsnip, potato and onion slices, overlapping in a shallow, greased baking dish. Dot with butter and sprinkle with some of the garlic and grated cheese, and salt and pepper.

3. Pour over one-quarter of the cream. Continue with these layers until all of the ingredients are used up. Finish with a layer of cheese and the remaining cream.

4. Bake at 190ºC (375ºF) Mark 5 for 1 hour or until tender. Transfer to a preheated grill to brown.

Parsnip & Apple Soup

Serves 6   Preparation 15 minutes   Cooking time 40 minutes

1 large onion

2 tbsp oil

500g (1lb) cooking apples

750g (1½lb) parsnips

900ml (1½ pints) vegetable stock

3 tbsp fresh parsley

600ml (1 pint) milk

Salt and pepper

1. Chop the onion and sauté in the hot oil until transparent.

2. Roughly chop the apples and parsnips and add to the pan. Continue to cook for 2 minutes.

3. Add the stock and chopped parsley and bring to the boil.

Season with salt and pepper. Cover and simmer for 30 minutes.

4. Stir in the milk. Transfer to a liquidiser and blend until smooth.

Parsnip Gratin

Serves 4   Preparation 15 minutes   Cooking time 50 minutes

750g (1½lb) parsnips

600ml (1 pint) apple juice

Juice of 1 lemon

6cm (3 inch) cinnamon stick

1 tbsp brown sugar

2 tbsp oil

Salt and pepper

1. Wash and roughly chop the parsnips and place in a shallow pan. Add the apple juice and lemon juice to half fill the pan.

2. Add the crushed cinnamon stick and season with salt and pepper. Bring to the boil, cover and cook gently for 40 minutes until tender.

3. Transfer to a shallow gratin dish and sprinkle with sugar. Drizzle over the oil and grill until brown.

65

Peas

Peas are prehistoric - cultivated and eaten before history was written. Dried peas used to be part of our staple diet as in pease pudding or pease porridge. Today, we eat them fresh and if you can pick them when they are young and sweet they can be eaten raw.

Peas are often cooked with mint. Add a sprig of mint to the steamer and serve as a side dish with a generous knob of butter. Or use chopped mint, as in these pasta sauce and soup recipes.

Pea, Broccoli & Mint Pasta Sauce

Serves 4   Preparation 15 minutes   Cooking time 15 minutes

1 medium onion

2 tbsp olive oil

250g (8oz) broccoli

250g (8oz) shelled peas

300ml (10fl oz) double cream

100g (4oz) ricotta cheese

2 tbsp fresh mint

Salt and pepper

1. Thinly slice the onion and sauté in hot oil until the onion is transparent.

2. Cut the broccoli into small florets and finely slice the stems. Add to the pan and fry for 3 minutes, stirring occasionally.

3. Add the peas and cook for a further 2 minutes.

4. Pour in the cream and cook gently for 5 minutes until the vegetables are just tender.

5. Stir in the ricotta cheese and finely chopped mint. Season with salt and pepper.

6. Serve with freshly cooked fusilli.

Pease Pudding

Serves 4   Preparation 15 minutes   Cooking time 60 minutes

1.5kg (3lb) peas in pods

3 tbsp fresh mint

50g (2oz) butter

Salt and pepper

Pinch of sugar

1. Shell the peas and place into a bowl lined with a piece of muslin.

2. Stir in 2 tablespoons of chopped mint, season with salt and pepper and add a pinch of sugar.

3. Tie up the muslin with string and place into a large pan of boiling water or weak vegetable stock. Cover and cook for 1 hour.

4. Lift the pudding out of the pan and put in a colander for a few minutes to drain. Untie the bag, transfer to a liquidiser and purée roughly.

5. Return to the muslin and reform into a round ball. Turn on to a serving dish. It may then be left to cool and served cold.

6. Alternatively, heat the butter, add the remaining chopped mint and pour over the pudding whilst hot. Serve immediately.

Pea & Cucumber Soup

Serves 4   Preparation 15 minutes   Cooking time 30 minutes

1 large onion

2 garlic cloves

3 tbsp oil

1 cucumber

450ml (¾ pint) vegetable stock

3 tbsp fresh mint

250g (8oz) shelled peas

Salt and pepper

1. Chop the onion and garlic and sauté in hot oil until the onion is transparent.

2. Add the chopped cucumber, stock and chopped mint. Bring to the boil, cover and simmer for 20 minutes.

3. Transfer to a liquidiser and blend until smooth. Return to the pan.

4. Add the peas, season with salt and pepper and continue to simmer for 10 minutes until the peas are tender.

Peppers

Although peppers are related to chillies, they are not hot - even the seeds. Red peppers are ripened green peppers and taste the sweetest, especially when roasted. To roast, cut into quarters, brush with oil and bake in a very hot oven for 30 minutes.

You really need to grow peppers in a greenhouse where the plants will grow about 3 feet high, unless the red spider mite gets there first. You could take a chance on us having a hot summer, but there's not much danger of even growing a suntan in the UK.

Red Pepper Soup

Serves 6   Preparation 20 minutes   Cooking time 25 minutes

4 red peppers

1 large onion

250g (8oz) potatoes

2 garlic cloves

2 tbsp oil

1 x 400g (14oz) can tomatoes

900ml (1½ pints) vegetable stock

3 tbsp fresh basil

Salt and pepper

1. Cut the peppers into quarters and remove the core and seeds. Place on a baking tray skin side up and brush with olive oil. Cook under a hot grill for 5-10 minutes until the peppers are tender and the skin blistered. Allow to cool and remove any blackened skin.

2. Roughly chop the onion and potatoes and sauté in hot oil along with the crushed garlic until the onion is transparent. Add the peppers and continue cooking for a few minutes.

3. Stir in the tomatoes and the stock and season with salt and pepper. Bring to the boil, cover and simmer for 20 minutes, until the vegetables are tender.

4. Transfer to a liquidiser, add the fresh basil and blend until smooth.

Green Pepper & Tomato Salad

Serves 4   Preparation 15 minutes

2 green peppers

4 medium tomatoes

½ cucumber

4 spring onions

1 red chilli

For the dressing:

6 tbsp yoghurt

2 tbsp olive oil

1 garlic clove

1 tbsp fresh mint

Salt and pepper

1. Finely slice the peppers, tomatoes and cucumber and mix them together. Add the chopped spring onions and finely chopped red chilli.

2. Combine the yoghurt, oil, crushed garlic, chopped mint and salt and pepper in a screw-topped jar and shake vigorously. Pour the dressing over the salad.

Peppers with Pasta

Serves 4   Preparation 10 minutes   Cooking time 30 minutes

6 peppers (red, green & yellow)

150ml (6fl oz) olive oil

4 tbsp red wine vinegar

25g (1oz) sugar

Salt and pepper

1. Slice the peppers into long strips. Heat the oil, stir in the peppers and simmer, covered for 30 minutes.

2. Remove the pan from the heat and stir in the vinegar and sugar. Season with salt and pepper.

3. Serve with freshly cooked tagliatelle.

Hot Stuffed Green Peppers

Serves 4   Preparation 25 minutes   Cooking time 50 minutes

1 small onion

3 celery stalks

2 dried red chillies

2 garlic cloves

3 tbsp oil

250g (8oz) tomatoes

280g (10oz) cooked rice

175g (6oz) Gruyère cheese

6 green peppers

Salt and pepper

1. Finely chop the onions, celery, chillies and garlic and sauté in the hot oil for 5 minutes.

2. Chop the tomatoes and add to the pan. Cover and simmer for 10 minutes.

3. Remove the pan from the heat and stir in the cooked rice and grated cheese.

4. Slice the tops off the peppers and remove the seeds. Fill with the rice mixture and replace the tops. Bake at 180°C (350°F) Mark 4 for 35-40 minutes.

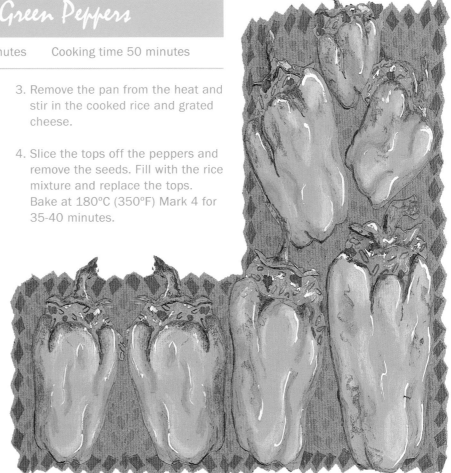

Potatoes

Probably the cheapest and most readily available of all organic vegetables, potatoes are also the most versatile. They used to be feared as the work of the devil because they grew underground, but whether served as an accompaniment or main course they are now a daily dish.

What else can I say about potatoes? I love chips and the other 1000 ways there are of preparing them, even boiled alone they can be superb. And you will probably find another 50 recipes in this book that include potatoes.

Spicy Potatoes with Onions

Serves 4   Preparation 15 minutes   Cooking time 30 minutes

1kg (2lb) potatoes

500g (1lb) onions

2 garlic cloves

2 tbsp oil

1 tsp ground turmeric

1 tsp ground coriander

1 tsp ground cumin

75g (3oz) raisins

2 tbsp fresh coriander

Salt and pepper

1. Cut the potatoes into 2cm (1 inch) cubes, boil for 10 minutes until just tender. Drain.

2. Meanwhile, finely chop the onions, crush the garlic and fry together for 10 minutes until the onion is transparent. Add the turmeric, ground coriander and cumin and continue frying for 2 minutes.

3. To this onion mixture, add the cooked potatoes and 5 tablespoons of water. Season with salt and pepper. Simmer gently for 10 minutes.

4. Add the raisins and continue to simmer for 10 minutes until the potatoes are soft and the sauce has thickened.

5. Just before serving add the chopped fresh coriander.

Roasted New Potatoes with Shallots

Serves 4
Preparation 15 minutes
Cooking time 45 minutes

750g (1½lb) new potatoes

3 tbsp olive oil

500g (1lb) shallots

1 tbsp balsamic vinegar

½ tsp sugar

Salt and pepper

1. Wash the potatoes, mix with the oil and place in a roasting tray.

2. Peel the shallots, cut into quarters and mix with the balsamic vinegar and sugar. Add to the roasting tray.

3. Season with salt and pepper and bake at 200°C (400°F) Mark 6 for 45 minutes until golden brown.

Potato, Courgette & Feta Cheese Gratin

Serves 4   Preparation 20 minutes   Cooking time 40 minutes

1kg (2lb) potatoes

2 tbsp oil

1 medium onion

2 medium courgettes

200g (7oz) feta cheese

450ml (¾ pint) milk

50g (2oz) cheddar cheese

1. Wash the potatoes and cut into 1cm (½ inch) slices. Boil for 5 minutes until just tender. Drain.

2. Meanwhile, slice the onion and sauté in hot oil for 5 minutes. Slice the courgettes, add to the pan and continue cooking for a further 5 minutes until just tender and lightly browned.

3. Mix the onion and courgettes with the potatoes and season with salt and pepper.

4. Cut the feta cheese into 1cm (½ inch) cubes and add to the potato mixture. Place into a shallow baking dish. Pour over the milk and sprinkle with the grated cheese. Bake for 30 minutes at 190°C (375°F) Mark 5.

Rosemary Potatoes

Serves 4
Preparation 10 minutes
Cooking time 45 minutes

1kg (2lb) potatoes

2 garlic cloves

2 tbsp fresh rosemary

3 tbsp olive oil

Salt and pepper

1. Wash the potatoes, chop into 1cm (½ inch) cubes and place in a large roasting tray.

2. Finely chop the garlic and rosemary and add to the potatoes. Mix in the olive oil and seasoning. Roast at 220°C (425°F) Mark 7 for 45 minutes, stirring half way through.

Potato & Onion Soup

Serves 6   Preparation 15 minutes   Cooking time 30 minutes

1 tbsp cumin seeds

2 tbsp oil

500g (1lb) onions

2 garlic cloves

500g (1lb) potatoes

600ml (1 pint) vegetable stock

150ml (5fl oz) white wine

300ml (½ pint) milk

Salt and pepper

1. Fry the cumin seeds in hot oil for a few seconds until they begin to pop. Roughly chop the onions, crush the garlic and add to the pan. Sauté for 10 minutes until the onion is transparent.

2. Roughly chop the potatoes and add to the pan along with the stock and white wine. Season with salt and pepper. Bring to the boil, cover and simmer for 20 minutes until the vegetables are tender.

3. Remove from the heat and stir in the milk. Transfer to a liquidiser and blend until smooth. Reheat gently before serving.

74

Potato Salad with Yoghurt & Herbs

Serves 6   Preparation 20 minutes   Cooking time 15 minutes

1kg (2lb) potatoes

3 eggs

240ml (8fl oz) plain yoghurt

6 tbsp olive oil

2 tbsp white wine vinegar

3 tbsp mixed fresh herbs
(e.g. parsley, mint, chives, dill)

Salt and pepper

1. Wash the potatoes and cut into
   2cm (1 inch) cubes. Cover them
   with cold water and boil for
   10-15 minutes until just tender.
   Drain.

2. Meanwhile, hardboil the eggs and
   run them under cold water. Peel,
   and mash them with a fork.

3. Mix the yoghurt with the olive oil
   and vinegar until blended. Finely
   chop the herbs and add to the
   yoghurt dressing. Season with salt
   and pepper.

4. Add the eggs to the yoghurt
   dressing and gently mix with the
   potatoes. Refrigerate until cold.

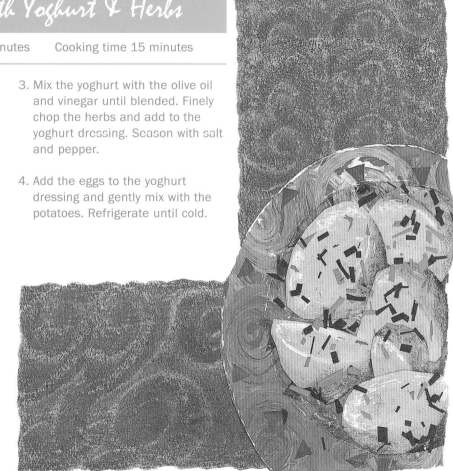

Pumpkin

Often grown to an enormous size to win prizes, always used for lanterns at Halloween and especially good for soups, pumpkins are the most popular of all squashes. If you grow your own and store them in a cold room they should keep until Christmas.

Pumpkins originally came from America where they are traditionally eaten at Thanksgiving to celebrate the harvest. There they are served as pumpkin pie, and I have included this sweet pie recipe here.

Pumpkin & Parsnip Gratin

Serves 4   Preparation 20 minutes   Cooking time 35 minutes

250g (8oz) parsnips

500g (1lb) pumpkin

1 medium onion

100g (4oz) cheddar cheese

Salt and pepper

2 tbsp fresh parsley

150ml (5fl oz) milk

150ml (5fl oz) single cream

1. Peel and cut the parsnips into ½cm (¼ inch) thick slices. Peel the pumpkin, remove the seeds and cut into ½cm (¼ inch) pieces. Slice the onion. Mix the vegetables together.

2. Place half of the vegetables in a greased, shallow baking dish. Grate the cheese and chop the parsley. Sprinkle half of each on top of the vegetables. Put the remaining vegetables on top and finish with the remaining cheese and parsley.

3. Pour over the milk and cream and bake at 180°C (350°F) Mark 4 for 35 minutes.

Pumpkin Pie

Serves 6   Preparation 25 minutes   Cooking time 60 minutes

For the shortcrust pastry:

175g (6oz) plain flour

Pinch of salt

75g (3oz) margarine

2 tbsp cold water

For the filling:

500g (1lb) pumpkin

100g (4oz) brown sugar

½ tsp ground ginger

1 tsp ground cinnamon

½ tsp ground mixed spice

3 eggs

150ml (5fl oz) single cream

1. Sift the flour and salt into a bowl. Cut the margarine into small pieces and rub into the flour until the mixture resembles fine breadcrumbs. Add 2 tablespoons of cold water to mix to a firm dough, then wrap in cling film and chill for 30 minutes.

2. Meanwhile, to prepare the filling, peel and dice the pumpkin flesh into 2cm (1 inch) chunks. Steam for 10 minutes until tender. Drain, transfer to a liquidiser and blend until smooth.

3. Put the pumpkin in a mixing bowl and beat in the remaining ingredients with an electric or hand whisk.

4. Roll out the pastry on a lightly floured surface to line a 20cm (8 inch) flan dish. Prick entire surface with a fork and bake blind at 190ºC (375ºF) Mark 5 for 15 minutes until just firm to the touch.

5. Pour the pumpkin mixture into the pastry base and bake at 190ºC (375ºF) Mark 5 for 45-50 minutes until set.

Roasted Pumpkin

Serves 4
Preparation 15 minutes
Cooking time 60 minutes

750g (1½lb) pumpkin

2 garlic cloves

1 tbsp fresh thyme leaves

4 tbsp olive oil

Salt and pepper

1. Peel the pumpkin, chop into 2cm (1 inch) wedges and place in a large roasting tray.

2. Finely chop the garlic and add to the pumpkin. Add the thyme leaves and olive oil and stir well to mix. Season with salt and pepper.

3. Roast at 200°C (400°F) Mark 6 for 60 minutes.

Pumpkin Soup

Serves 6   Preparation 15 minutes   Cooking time 20 minutes

1 medium onion

2 garlic cloves

6 tbsp oil

1.5kg (3lb) pumpkin

2 bay leaves

300 ml (½ pint) milk

300 ml (½ pint) single cream

Salt and pepper

1. Chop the onion, crush the garlic and sauté in the hot oil until the onion is transparent.

2. Peel the pumpkin and cut into 1cm (½ inch) pieces. Add to the onion along with the bay leaves, salt and pepper. Cover and cook for 15 minutes until the pumpkin is soft.

3. Transfer to a liquidiser, add the milk and blend until smooth. Add the cream and reheat gently before serving.

Spinach

You can grow spinach, in its many varieties, all year round. Although "perpetual spinach" is really a type of beetroot and is usually better cooked, summer varieties are very nutritious served raw in salads.

It is not always easy to get children to eat their greens. But this Spinach & Pea Soup is a brilliant green colour and even our three year old enjoys it.

As it reduces so much during cooking you should allow about 500g (1lb) of spinach per person and cram it into your largest pan.

Spinach & Pea Soup

Serves 6   Preparation 15 minutes   Cooking time 40 minutes

2 medium potatoes

1 medium onion

1 garlic clove

2 tbsp oil

1 tsp ground cumin

500g (1lb) spinach

2 tbsp fresh mint

250g (8oz) shelled peas

1.2 liters (2 pints) vegetable stock

1 tsp grated nutmeg

Salt and pepper

1. Roughly chop the potatoes and onion and crush the garlic. Sauté in the hot oil until the onion is transparent. Stir in the cumin and continue to cook for a further 2 minutes.

2. Wash and shred the spinach (including stalks) and chop the mint. Add the spinach, mint, peas and stock to the pan.

3. Bring to the boil, cover and simmer gently for 25 minutes. Transfer to a liquidiser and blend until smooth. Season with salt, pepper and nutmeg. Reheat before serving.

Spinach & Feta Filo Pie

Serves 6   Preparation 30 minutes   Cooking time 30 minutes

500g (1lb) spinach

½ tsp freshly grated nutmeg

200g (7oz) feta cheese

500g (1lb) tomatoes

1 tbsp fresh mint

75g (3oz) butter

250g (8oz) pack filo pastry

1 tbsp sunflower seeds

1. Wash the spinach and heat in a large pan until it wilts. Sprinkle with the nutmeg.

2. Crumble the feta cheese and mix with the spinach. Chop the tomatoes into 1cm (1/2 inch) pieces and add to the spinach along with the chopped mint.

3. Brush a deep, 28cm x 23cm (11 inches x 9 inches) roasting tin with melted butter. Open out the pastry and cut in half. Keep the pastry that you are not working with covered to prevent it from drying out.

4. Lay one sheet of pastry in the tin, brush with butter and lay another sheet on top. Repeat until there are eight layers.

5. Spread a quarter of the spinach mixture over the pastry. Lay another three buttered sheets on top. Repeat to give four layers.

6. Top with three more buttered sheets. Scrunch up the remaining sheets and scatter on top. Pour the remaining butter over the pie and sprinkle with sunflower seeds.

7. Bake at 200°C (400°F) Mark 6 for 25-30 minutes until golden brown.

Stir-Fried Spinach

Serves 4
Preparation 10 minutes
Cooking time 3 minutes

1kg (2 lb) spinach

2 garlic cloves

2 tbsp oil

1 tbsp lemon juice

Salt and pepper

1. Wash and roughly chop the spinach.

2. Heat the oil in a large pan, add the finely chopped garlic and stir-fry for a few seconds. Add the spinach and continue to stir-fry for 2-3 minutes.

3. Add in the lemon juice and season with salt and pepper.

Spinach with Potatoes

Serves 4   Preparation 20 minutes   Cooking time 30 minutes

1kg (2lb) potatoes

1 large onion

2 garlic cloves

1 tsp black mustard seeds

6 tbsp oil

500g (1lb) spinach

1 tsp ground cumin

1 tsp garam masala

Salt and pepper

1. Wash the potatoes and cut into 1cm (½ inch) cubes. Place in a pan of water and boil for 10 minutes until just tender. Drain.

2. Chop the onion and the garlic. Put the mustard seeds into the hot oil, stir for a few seconds and add the onion and garlic. Fry gently for 5 minutes until the onion is lightly browned.

3. Add the finely chopped spinach and continue cooking for 10 minutes, stirring frequently.

4. Add the cumin, garam masala and potatoes. Season with salt and pepper and heat through.

Spinach & Blue Cheese Pasta Sauce

Serves 4   Preparation 15 minutes   Cooking time 15 minutes

500g (1lb) spinach

1 medium onion

1 garlic clove

2 tbsp olive oil

1 tbsp flour

450ml (¾ pint) milk

100g (4oz) blue cheese

Salt and pepper

1. Chop the spinach and steam for 5-10 minutes until tender.

2. Chop the onion and sauté in hot oil with the crushed garlic for 5 minutes. Add the flour and cook for 1 minute. Gradually add the milk and stir until thickened. Simmer gently for 3 minutes.

3. Crumble the cheese and add to the sauce. Stir in the spinach and season with salt and pepper. Cook, stirring until the cheese has melted.

4. Serve with freshly cooked fettucine.

Squash

There are many different types of squash, but they are interchangeable in most recipes. Pumpkins are the best known (see Pumpkin) and easily substitute for Acorn or Butternut squashes. They all have a mild flavour and go well with herbs and spices.

Try baking small squashes whole, removing the seeds when cooked and serving with herb butter, salt and pepper. Patty Pan Squash (flat with frilly edges) can be sliced and fried with garlic or cooked like courgettes. Have fun with Spaghetti Squash.

Squash & Chick Pea Soup

Serves 6   Preparation 20 minutes   Cooking time 50 minutes

1.25kg (2½lb) butternut squash

1 large onion

2 garlic cloves

3 tbsp oil

1 x 400g (14oz) can chick peas

1 dried red chilli

1 tsp ground cumin

1 tsp ground coriander

1.2 litres (2 pints) vegetable stock

2 x 400g (14oz) cans tomatoes

Salt and pepper

1. Peel the squash, scrape out the seeds and chop into 2cm (1 inch) pieces.

2. Chop the onion and garlic and sauté in hot oil for 5 minutes.

3. Add the squash to the pan and continue to cook for 5 minutes, stirring frequently. Finely chop the chilli and add to the squash mixture along with the cumin and coriander and cook for a further 2 minutes.

4. Stir in the stock, chopped tomatoes and drained chick peas. Season with salt and pepper. Bring to the boil, cover and simmer for 35 minutes until the squash is tender.

5. Transfer to a liquidiser and blend until smooth.

Roasted Squash

Serves 4
Preparation 10 minutes
Cooking time 45 minutes

---

2 large spaghetti squash

100g (4oz) butter

1 tbsp fresh chives

2 tbsp fresh thyme leaves

1. Cut the squash in half lengthways, remove seeds and place cut side up on a baking tray.

2. Chop the chives, add to the thyme leaves and mix with the softened butter.

3. Spread the butter over the squash, cover with foil and bake at 220°C (425°F) Mark 7 for 45 minutes. Remove the foil for the last 15 minutes of cooking time.

Butternut Squash Stir-Fry

Serves 4   Preparation 20 minutes   Cooking time 15 minutes

750g (1½lb) butternut squash

250g (8oz) carrots

1 bunch spring onions

1 large onion

2 garlic cloves

4cm (2 inch) piece root ginger

1 dried red chilli

5 tbsp oil

50g (2oz) sesame seeds

4 tbsp fresh coriander

5 tbsp soy sauce

1. Peel the squash, remove the seeds and chop into 1cm (½ inch) cubes. Finely slice the carrots, spring onions and onion. Crush the garlic, peel and grate the root ginger and finely chop the chilli.

2. Dry-fry the sesame seeds in a small frying pan, stirring frequently.

3. Fry the onion and garlic in hot oil for 5 minutes. Add the squash, carrots, spring onions, ginger and chilli and stir-fry for a further 5 minutes until the squash is just tender.

4. Stir in the sesame seeds, chopped coriander and soy sauce.

5. Serve with freshly cooked noodles.

Swiss Chard

Swiss chard, a type of leaf beet, is very easy to grow and unlikely to bolt. Ruby chard and rainbow chard have brightly coloured stems but all types can be used in these recipes.

You can cook chard as you would spinach. But, unless the leaves are young and small, you should separate the stems from the green part and cooked them for longer.

Don't be tempted to discard a lot of stem, they are delicious and some people grow chard for the stem alone.

Swiss Chard & Potato Gratin

Serves 4   Preparation 25 minutes   Cooking time 55 minutes

500g (1lb) Swiss chard

750g (1½lb) potatoes

75g (3oz) margarine

4 garlic cloves

2 tbsp plain flour

600ml (1 pint) milk

100g (4oz) cheddar cheese

Salt and pepper

1. Remove and roughly chop the green part of the chard leaves. Cut the stalks into 2cm (1 inch) lengths and steam for 10 minutes. Stir in the green leaves and continue to cook for a few minutes.

2. Wash the potatoes and cut into 1cm (½ inch) slices. Boil for 5 minutes until just tender. Drain.

3. Grease a shallow baking dish and layer with half of the potatoes, the chard and then the remaining potatoes.

4. To make the sauce, melt the margarine and fry the crushed garlic for 2 minutes. Stir in the flour and continue stirring for 1 minute. Gradually add the milk, stirring continuously until the sauce thickens. Add half the grated cheese and season with salt and pepper.

5. Pour the sauce over the vegetables and top with the remaining cheese. Bake at 180°C (350°F) Mark 4 for 35 minutes.

Swiss Chard with Chick Peas

Serves 4   preparation 20 minutes   Cooking time 20 minutes

1 medium onion

4 tbsp oil

2 garlic cloves

2 tsp cumin seeds

3 large tomatoes

750g (1½lb) Swiss chard

300ml (½ pint) vegetable stock

1 x 400g (14oz) can chick peas

50g (2oz) raisins

Salt and pepper

1. Finely slice the onion and sauté in hot oil for 5 minutes. Add the crushed garlic and cumin seeds and fry for 1 minute.

2. Chop the tomatoes, add to the pan and cook for a further 5 minutes.

3. Shred the green of the swiss chard, chop the centre stalk and add to the pan. Pour in the stock, drained chick peas and raisins, season with salt and pepper and simmer for 10 minutes.

Swiss Chard Pasta Sauce

Serves 4   Preparation 15 minutes   Cooking time 30 minutes

750g (1½lb) Swiss chard

1 large onion

4 garlic cloves

5 tbsp olive oil

150ml (5fl oz) double cream

100g (4oz) Parmesan cheese

Salt and pepper

1. Roughly chop the chard and steam for 10 minutes until tender.

2. Slice the onion, crush the garlic and fry together for 15 minutes until the onion is soft and browned.

3. Add the chard to the pan and stir in the cream. Season with salt and pepper. Add the grated Parmesan.

4. Serve with freshly cooked farfalle.

Tomatoes

Tomatoes are a versatile and frequently used ingredient and you can grow your own outdoors even in our summers. They taste best fresh from your vine rather than the supermarket. And although tinned organic tomatoes are now readily available they can't always be used as a substitute for fresh ones.

Tomatoes come in many shapes and sizes but any will do for these recipes. Cherry tomatoes are the sweetest and are perfect for Roasted Tomato & Feta Pasta Sauce and Tomato & Feta Cheese Tart.

Classic Tomato Sauce

Makes 600ml (1 pint)   Preparation 35 minutes   Cooking time 30 minutes

1.5kg (3lb) tomatoes

1 small onion

1 garlic clove

3 tbsp olive oil

1 tbsp fresh marjoram

Salt and pepper

1. Skin the tomatoes by placing in a bowl and pouring over boiling water to cover. Leave for 30 seconds, lift out and remove skin. To make a rich sauce the tomatoes should be seeded. To remove the seeds, hold the tomato under running water and scoop out the seeds with a teaspoon. Chop roughly.

2. Finely chop the onion and garlic and fry in hot oil for 5 minutes until softened.

3. Add the tomatoes, cover and cook for 25 minutes, stirring frequently. Add the marjoram 10 minutes before the end of cooking time. Season with salt and pepper.

4. Serve as an accompaniment to meat or vegetables or as a pasta sauce for four.

Tomato & Courgette Gratin

Serves 4   Preparation 15 minutes   Cooking time 50 minutes

500g (1lb) tomatoes

250g (8oz) courgettes

250g (8oz) potatoes

1 medium onion

2 tbsp fresh marjoram

3 tbsp olive oil

50g (2oz) Cheddar cheese

1. Slice the tomatoes, courgettes, potatoes and onion into ½cm (¼ inch) slices. Chop the fresh marjoram.

2. Arrange the vegetables in layers in an ovenproof dish, sprinkling with the marjoram throughout.

3. Pour over the olive oil and top with grated cheese. Bake at 180ºC (350ºF) Mark 4 for 50 minutes until golden brown.

Tomato & Basil Soup

Serves 6   Preparation 10 minutes   Cooking time 30 minutes

1kg (2lb) tomatoes

2 medium onions

500g (1lb) carrots

900ml (1½ pints) vegetable stock

1 tbsp tomato purée

4 tbsp fresh basil

Salt and pepper

1. Roughly chop the tomatoes and onions and slice the carrots. Place in a large pan along with the stock and tomato purée. Bring to the boil, cover and simmer for 30 minutes until the vegetables are tender.

2. Transfer to a liquidiser and blend until smooth. Stir in the chopped basil and season with salt and pepper.

Tomato Salad

Serves 4   Preparation 15 minutes

500g (1lb) tomatoes

2 tbsp fresh basil

2 tbsp fresh chives

2 tbsp pine nuts

1 garlic clove

6 tbsp olive oil

2 tbsp white wine vinegar

1. Wash and slice the tomatoes and mix with the chopped fresh herbs and crushed garlic.

2. Spread the pine nuts onto a baking tray and grill until lightly browned. Be careful not to burn them.

3. Combine the oil and vinegar in a screw-topped jar and shake to mix. Pour the dressing over the tomato salad and sprinkle with the pine nuts. Refrigerate until cold.

Roasted Tomato & Feta Pasta Sauce

Serves 4   Preparation 15 minutes   Cooking time 30 minutes

750g (1½lb) tomatoes

3 garlic cloves

8 tbsp olive oil

200g (7oz) feta cheese

3 tbsp fresh basil

Salt and pepper

1. Chop the tomatoes into 1cm (½ inch) chunks. Crush the garlic, add to the tomatoes and place in a shallow roasting tray. Pour on the oil and stir to mix. Roast at 200°C (400°F) Mark 6 for 30 minutes.

2. Meanwhile, cut the feta cheese into 1cm (½ inch) cubes and mix with the shredded basil.

3. Mix the roasted tomatoes with the feta and season with salt and pepper.

4. Serve with freshly cooked farfalle.

Tomato & Feta Cheese Tart

Serves 6   Preparation 25 minutes   Cooking time 30 minutes

For the shortcrust pastry:

175g (6oz) plain flour

Pinch of salt

75g (3oz) margarine

2 tbsp cold water

For the filling:

200g (7oz) feta cheese

100g (4oz) black olives

2 tbsp fresh basil

500g (1lb) tomatoes

1 garlic clove

1 tbsp olive oil

1. Sift the flour and salt into a bowl. Cut the margarine into small pieces and rub into the flour until the mixture resembles fine breadcrumbs. Add 2 tablespoons of cold water to mix to a firm dough, then wrap in cling film and chill for 30 minutes.

2. Meanwhile, to prepare the filling, mash up the feta cheese and mix with the chopped olives. Finely chop the basil and add to the cheese mixture.

3. Cut the tomatoes into 1cm (½ inch) chunks and mix with the olive oil.

4. Roll out the pastry on a lightly floured surface to line a 20cm (8 inch) flan dish. Prick entire surface with a fork and bake blind at 200°C (400°F) Mark 6 for 15 minutes until just firm to the touch.

5. Spread the feta cheese mixture over the pastry case and spread the tomatoes on top. Bake at 200°C (400°F) Mark 6 for 20 minutes.

Turnips

Turnips are an easy and quick to grow crop but you may have already been put off them as an overcooked mush in school dinners. Once grown mainly for cattle food, they can also be fit for human consumption.

Pick them when they are the size of a golf ball and eat raw, grated in salads or steam whole until tender. Do try these baby ones in an orange glaze.

Peel and dice older turnips to add to soups and casseroles or mash them with plenty of butter, cream, pepper and a dash of lemon.

Turnip & Potato Gratin

Serves 4   Preparation 15 minutes   Cooking time 55 minutes

500g (1lb) turnips

500g (1lb) potatoes

1 medium onion

2 tbsp oil

150ml (5fl oz) milk

1 tsp grated nutmeg

50g (2oz) cheddar cheese

Salt and pepper

1. Peel the turnips and cut into ½ cm (¼ inch) slices. Also cut the potatoes and onion into ½ cm (¼ inch) slices.

2. Mix these vegetables with the oil and place in an ovenproof dish. Cover tightly and bake at 190ºC (375ºF) Mark 5 for 30 minutes.

3. Pour the milk into a small pan, season with freshly grated nutmeg, salt and pepper and bring to the boil. Remove from heat.

4. Remove the turnip mixture from the oven, mix in half of the cheese and pour the milk on top. Sprinkle with the remaining cheese and return to the oven, uncovered, for a further 25 minutes until golden brown.

Orange Glazed Turnips

Serves 4   Preparation 15 minutes   Cooking time 20 minutes

1kg (2lb) baby turnips

1 tsp coriander seeds

50g (2oz) butter

1 tbsp sugar

Grated rind of 1 orange

150ml (5fl oz) vegetable stock

1 tbsp orange juice

2 tbsp fresh coriander

Salt and pepper

1. Wash the turnips and place in a pan of boiling water for 5 minutes until barely tender. Drain.

2. Melt the butter in a large frying pan and add the crushed coriander seeds. Add the turnips, sugar and orange rind and sauté for 5 minutes, stirring, until the turnips are beginning to brown.

3. Pour in the stock and season with salt and pepper. Simmer on a high heat until the sauce thickens. Stir in the orange juice and chopped coriander.

Watercress

Watercress needs to be grown in fresh, flowing water beds - not easy in a back garden. But land cress is an alternative and you can use it in the same way.

Watercress has a distinctive peppery flavour and is delicious in this soup. Watercress soufflé should have a light texture and it is worth the trouble, but you will have to sprint from oven to table.

Avoid limp, yellow leaves and store your watercress in a jar of water in the fridge to keep it fresh.

Watercress Soufflé

Serves 4   Preparation 30 minutes   Cooking time 30 minutes

1 bunch watercress

25g (1oz) margarine

25g (1oz) flour

300ml (½ pint) milk

50g (2oz) cheddar cheese

4 large eggs

Salt and pepper

1. Wash and finely chop the watercress.

2. Melt the margarine, add the flour and cook, stirring for 1 minute. Slowly add the milk and continue stirring until the sauce thickens. Remove from the heat and stir in the grated cheese. Season with salt and pepper.

3. Separate the eggs and beat the yolks into the white sauce. Stir in the watercress.

4. Whisk the egg whites until stiff and fold into the sauce. Pour into a greased soufflé dish and bake at 200°C (400°F) Mark 6 for 25 minutes until firm and golden brown. Serve immediately.

Watercress Pasta Sauce

Serves 4   Preparation 10 minutes   Cooking time 15 minutes

1 medium onion

1 garlic clove

2 tbsp olive oil

100g (4oz) mushrooms

100g (4oz) walnuts

1 bunch watercress

240ml (8fl oz) yoghurt

Salt and pepper

1. Chop the onion and garlic and sauté in the hot oil until the onion is transparent.

2. Slice the mushrooms, chop the walnuts and add to the pan. Cook for a further 3 minutes. Stir in the chopped watercress and sauté gently until soft.

3. Stir in the yoghurt. Season with salt and pepper and serve with freshly cooked tagliatelle.

Watercress Soup

Serves 4   Preparation 15 minutes   Cooking time 25 minutes

1 medium onion

250g (8oz) potatoes

2 tbsp oil

1 bunch watercress

600ml (1 pint) vegetable stock

150ml (5fl oz) milk

½ tsp grated nutmeg

Salt and pepper

1. Chop the onion and potatoes and sauté in hot oil until the onion is transparent. Add the chopped watercress and cook for a further 3 minutes.

2. Add the stock, nutmeg and seasoning. Cover and simmer gently for 20 minutes until the potato is soft.

3. Cool slightly and blend in a liquidiser until smooth. Stir in the milk and reheat gently before serving.

Basics

This final set of recipes is designed to use the basics - carrots, onions and potatoes. And some of the root vegetables which you can swop around - swede, parsnips and turnips.

Spicy Vegetable Casserole uses whole spices and it is worth dry-frying them and crushing rather than using the ready-ground ones - they smell wonderful.

Vegetable Stir-Fry can be adapted with the addition of almost anything, and if you have some sherry hanging around add a big splash.

Winter Ratatouille

Serves 4   Preparation 15 minutes   Cooking time 40 minutes

2 medium onions

2 garlic cloves

4 tbsp oil

3 medium carrots

2 large parsnips

3 sticks of celery

500g (1lb) turnip or swede

1 tsp dried sage

2 tsp dried thyme

Salt and pepper

1. Chop the onion and garlic and sauté in the hot oil until the onion is transparent.

2. Wash and chop the carrots, parsnips and celery into 2cm (1 inch) chunks. Peel and chop the turnip. Add the chopped vegetables to the pan and fry for 5 minutes.

3. Add the herbs and season with salt and pepper. Cover and cook gently for 30 minutes until the vegetables are tender, stirring occasionally.

Hot Roasted Roots

Serves 4   Preparation 25 minutes   Cooking time 60 minutes

4 medium carrots

2 leeks

2 sticks celery

250g (8oz) swede

1 large onion

6 garlic cloves

2cm (1 inch) piece root ginger

1 tsp cumin seeds

1 tsp coriander seeds

4 tbsp oil

Salt and pepper

1. Wash and chop the carrots, leeks and celery into 2cm (1 inch) chunks. Peel and chop the swede and onion. Peel and finely chop the garlic and ginger. Mix these ingredients in a large roasting tray.

2. Lightly crush the cumin and coriander seeds and sprinkle over the top. Season with salt and pepper.

3. Drizzle over the oil. Roast in a preheated oven at 200°C (400°F) Mark 6 for 60 minutes stirring occasionally.

Spicy Vegetable Casserole

Serves 6   Preparation 30 minutes   Cooking time 35 minutes

1 large onion

3 garlic cloves

1 dried red chilli

2 tbsp oil

1 tsp cumin seeds

2 tsp coriander seeds

1 tbsp sesame seeds

500g (1lb) butternut squash

2 courgettes

1 red pepper

1 green pepper

3 medium carrots

250g (8oz) potatoes

1 x 400g (14oz) can tomatoes

450ml (¾ pint) vegetable stock

250g (8oz) spinach

1. Chop the onion, crush the garlic and finely chop the red chilli. Sauté these in hot oil for 10 minutes until the onion is transparent.

2. Meanwhile, put the cumin, coriander and sesame seeds into a small pan and dry-fry for a few minutes until the seeds begin to pop. Crush with a pestle and mortar.

3. Add the seeds to the onion mixture and cook, stirring, for a few minutes.

4. Peel the squash, remove the seeds and chop into 2cm (1 inch) chunks. Cut the courgettes, peppers, carrots and potatoes into chunks. Add all of these vegetables to the pan and mix well.

5. Stir in the chopped tomatoes and stock. Bring to the boil, cover and simmer for 25 minutes until vegetables are tender.

6. Roughly shred the spinach and stir into the casserole. Cook for a few minutes until the spinach is tender.

Vegetable Stir-Fry

Serves 4   Preparation 20 minutes   Cooking time 10 minutes

2 medium carrots

2 medium courgettes

1 red pepper

½ small white cabbage

100g (4oz) mushrooms

1 small head broccoli

1 medium onion

2cm (1 inch) piece root ginger

2 garlic cloves

4 tbsp oil

2 tbsp soy sauce

1. Cut the carrots and courgettes into matchstick sized pieces. Finely slice the pepper, cabbage and mushrooms. Break the broccoli into small florets and finely slice the stems. Mix these vegetables together in a large bowl.

2. Finely chop the onion, root ginger and garlic and fry in hot oil for 3 minutes.

3. Add all of the vegetables and stir-fry on a high heat for 5 minutes until the vegetables are just tender. Stir in the soy sauce.

4. Serve with freshly cooked noodles or rice.

Mulligatawny Soup

Serves 6   Preparation 15 minutes   Cooking time 40 minutes

2 medium carrots

2 medium onions

2 medium potatoes

1 large cooking apple

2 tbsp oil

2 garlic cloves

1 tbsp flour

1 tbsp curry powder

1.2 litres (2 pints) vegetable stock

300ml (½ pint) tomato juice

50g (2oz) sultanas

Salt and pepper

1. Roughly chop the vegetables and apple. Sauté in the hot oil for 10 minutes until the onion is transparent.

2. Add the crushed garlic and stir in the curry powder and flour. Cook, stirring for 2 minutes.

3. Gradually stir in the stock and tomato juice, bring to the boil and cook until thickened.

4. Add the sultanas and season with salt and pepper.

5. Cover and cook gently for 30 minutes. Cool slightly and blend in a liquidiser until smooth. Reheat gently before serving.

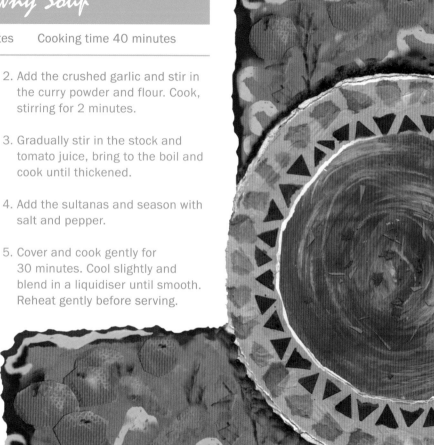

Root Vegetable Stew

Serves 4   Preparation 20 minutes   Cooking time 50 minutes

2 large onions

2 garlic cloves

3 tbsp oil

2 tsp coriander seeds

2 tsp cumin seeds

250g (8oz) carrots

250g (8oz) turnips

250g (8oz) swede

250g (8oz) parsnips

250g (8oz) split red lentils

900ml (1½ pints) vegetable stock

1 x 400g (14oz) can tomatoes

Salt and pepper

1. Chop the onions and sauté in hot oil with the crushed garlic, until the onion is transparent.

2. Meanwhile, put the coriander and cumin seeds into a small pan and dry-fry for a few minutes, stirring occasionally. Crush with a pestle and mortar.

3. Add the seeds to the onion mixture and cook, stirring, for 2 minutes.

4. Wash the carrots and slice into 2cm (1 inch) chunks. Peel and chop the turnip, swede and parsnips. Add these vegetables to the onion mixture and cook for a few minutes.

5. Wash the lentils, add to the pan and stir well to mix. Pour in the stock and chopped tomatoes. Season with salt and pepper.

6. Cover and simmer gently for 40 minutes until the vegetables are tender and the lentils are soft.

Vegetable Casserole

Serves 6   Preparation 20 minutes   Cooking time 2 hours

2 medium onions

500g (1lb) leeks

2 garlic cloves

2 tbsp oil

500g (1lb) potatoes

250g (8oz) carrots

250g (8oz) celeriac

250g (8oz) parsnips

250g (8oz) mushrooms

100g (4oz) pearl barley

1 x 400g (14oz) can tomatoes

2 tbsp tomato purée

900ml (1½ pints) vegetable stock

2 tbsp fresh parsley

Salt and pepper

1. Slice the onions and leeks and fry in hot oil with the crushed garlic for 10 minutes until softened.

2. Chop the potatoes, carrots, celeriac and parsnips into 2cm (1 inch) chunks and slice the mushrooms.

3. Place all of these vegetables into a large casserole dish, stir in the onion mixture and all of the remaining ingredients, except the parsley.

4. Cover the casserole and bake at 180°C (350°F) Mark 4 for 1½-2 hours until the vegetables are tender. Stir in the chopped fresh parsley.

Creamy Vegetable Bake

Serves 4   Preparation 20 minutes   Cooking time 1 hour 20 minutes

250g (8oz) parsnips

250g (8oz) swede

250g (8oz) celeriac

150ml (5fl oz) double cream

300ml (½ pint) milk

2 tbsp fresh parsley

2 tbsp fresh mint

2 garlic cloves

100g (4oz) cheddar cheese

4 tbsp oil

Salt and pepper

25g (1oz) butter

1. Peel and thinly slice the vegetables (use the slicing blade of a food processor if available).

2. Place in a large pan with the cream and milk. Bring to the boil and simmer for 2 minutes only.

3. Add the grated cheddar and stir until melted. Season with salt and pepper.

4. Finely chop the parsley, mint and garlic and mix together with the oil.

5. Put half of the vegetable mixture into a large baking dish and spread the oil mixture on top. Put the remaining vegetables on top and dot with the butter.

6. Cover with foil and bake at 200°C (400°F) Mark 6 for 50 minutes. Remove the foil and continue to cook for a further 30 minutes until the vegetables are tender.

Index